# DROPPING THE BELT

By David Farrell

&

Three Anonymous Ghostwriters

Also By David Farrell

*The Last Resort*

*The Glove*

*You Can't Get Rid of Me That Easily*

*Twelve*

Copyright © 2019 by David Farrell

All rights reserved.

This book or any portion thereof may not be reproduced or used in any manner whatsoever without the express written permission of the publisher except for the use of brief quotations in a book review.

Printed in Australia

First Printing 2019

Paperback ISBN:    978-1-64516-717-4
Digital ISBN:         978-1-64516-716-7

The *Infinite Monkey Theorem* poses the idea that an unlimited number of monkeys supplied with typewriters and sufficient time would eventually produce the complete works of William Shakespeare.

I provided three ghostwriters with one week each.

## PREFACE

It all started when I found out you could pay people online to ghostwrite your story ideas into novels or ebooks for you. Who were these Internet entities? It was impossible to know for sure but they presented themselves as anonymous writers. All I had to go on was a short profile on each writer and a picture. Were they as capable as they claimed? Were they even from English speaking countries? There were no writing samples available and I'll admit – I was kind of curious. As a part time writer I have a lot of half-formed ideas and the notion that someone else could help me develop one of them was appealing. I'd heard of ghostwriters penning books for celebrities. Why not for me? Yeah…I can tell what you're thinking and you're definitely right.

I *could* have just written it myself – I know! It goes against every code writers have really. But I was in the midst of completing another novel and so I decided to try it out. This would be my own little experiment.

I should introduce myself. Hi! My name is David Farrell and I'm a wannabe writer living in Melbourne, Australia. I'd done some filmmaking in Canberra where I grew up. After I completed my shoestring budget feature film *The Last Resort* I was contemplating my next project. While walking through the city I saw a flyer for a live professional wrestling show. I attended, met some of the wrestlers and a documentary project began. They were a fun eclectic group that had grown up loving wrestling. They were just more interested in being in front of the camera than I was.

The documentary was titled *The Young and the Wrestlers*. It was during the production of that very project that I had the idea for the novel *Dropping the Belt* that you're holding in your hands right now.

Randomly during an interview I remember one of the wrestlers telling me about how he'd taken a job as a topless waiter to get some extra cash. It was a throw away comment that never made it into the final film. It made sense really. These wrestlers are cocky showboats that are in good shape. It would have been a fun thing for them to do on the side. I imagined that they met lots of girls that way too. And so – in an odd way - the seed of an idea was planted.

Hypothetically what if a girl at a hen's night met a topless waiter such as my friend but didn't know their professional wrestling background until later? That seemed like a funny premise for a romantic comedy to me. I imagined the reveal of his secret world and allowing her behind the curtain.

Would his passion for wrestling complicate his relationship with her? Would she be accepting of such a bizarre and superficial world? Could the tale end in a way that made him choose between her and his career in wrestling? There were so many ways the story could go. It was a half formed idea that I held onto for years.

My own interest in wrestling stemmed from my childhood. My brother William and I would stay up late watching wrestling whenever Australian television channels deemed it worth scheduling. We would track its forever-changing timeslot for years at a time. We didn't have the luxury of Pay TV in our house. In our downtime we would play wrestling video games well into our twenties (alright…and early thirties!) inventing complicated storylines for the characters and stakes that only *we* were aware of. We custom made all of our favourite characters and then simulated matches between them. We would act as the General Manager of a famous brand like RAW or Smackdown and make decisions about everything from championship contenders to backstage storylines. I even made a wrestling board game at one point that I still own.

Yes, I'll admit I've always liked professional wrestling. Ironically it appeals to me because of the storylines and behind the scenes drama more than the actual competitive fights. I found interviews with wrestlers like The Rock, Stone Cold Steve Austin and Mick Foley were the highlight of the show. I loved the narrative. Why did these characters *want* to fight eachother? What was their motivation? Good and evil duking it out in the ring for a championship? Great. The actual wrestling was always a bonus. I often found myself fast-forwarding the wrestling I'd taped to see how a match ended. How would they parlay this match into the events of next week? Was the champion cheated out of a victory? Did someone interfere? How were they going to top *this* spectacle? The soap opera of it intrigued me the most, and wrestling was like a soap opera for men.

I don't really have time for filmmaking anymore and so these days I like to write. It's my way of scratching that creative itch. I have lots of ideas for stories and I'm always developing them in the background. The idea of using a ghostwriter was something I'd never considered before now. This felt like an interesting way of making a start on *Dropping the Belt* and seemed like a risk worth taking.

    The worst-case scenario would be if the ghostwriter ran away with my money into the depths of the Internet. That was a possibility. Maybe, if they were as advertised, I would have ten thousand words of a wrestling rom-com and the inspiration to rewrite it and continue it myself. What could go wrong really?

    If I only knew…

David Farrell

## PART ONE

When I found the website of potential ghostwriters I spent a long time reading their profiles and examining their claims. I decided on one with a decent price point ($25 for ten thousand words) that resided in America – the home of professional wrestling! Would this American male – aged between 25 and 35 according to their profile picture – be the man for the job? For that price did he just have a prewritten template that he would drop my idea into? This felt like it *could* be a trick based on the low price. Would he – if it *was* actually a he - deliver some unintelligible rubbish? Did he even want to write my silly half formed story? I put my idea down in words and decided to throw caution to the wind. All of the ghostwriters on the site ask you to contact them first in case they are too busy or not interested enough to work on your story. I learned pretty quickly that ghostwriters *want* work. They will probably write anything you ask them to. Money talks. Things started out with a simple message to see whether he was interested in the concept. Here is the transcript of our initial conversation.

ME:

Hi there. I just wanted to float a story your way and see if you are interested in writing it. It's a romantic / action / wrestling story. Ten thousand words. It's called *Dropping the Belt*. This is a wrestling term for losing a championship belt. It's about a woman (Ella) that meets a topless waiter (Hunter) at a hen's night and agrees to go on a date with him. They bond over a dinner and he seems great - except that he is a professional wrestler. The kind of wrestling where it's fake, but don't tell him that! She agrees to watch him wrestle and gets excited by the crowd and spectacle. Ella is cool with it and they start dating.

His character can be 'The Hunter' or something like that. With leopard print style attire that he wears in the ring.

He's an attractive guy (sandy blonde hair, in shape) and she worries about other women liking him. Hunter is on the road a fair bit for various wrestling gigs.

Eventually Ella fills in as his wrestling valet (ringside partner) and experiences an angry crowd. He's been a 'good guy' wrestler (known as a 'face') and he's turning bad (aka 'heel'). Hunter didn't tell Ella about the turn.

The wrestling promoters have agreed to make him the champion if he goes bad permanently. To get into character he starts acting like a rude guy at home and it bleeds into his day-to-day life with her. They break up and in the end he decides to 'drop the belt' (aka: lose the title) and walk away from the ring to be with her.

Ella can have some disapproving friends from the hen's night. They definitely don't understand wrestling. Hunter should have a roommate that is also a wrestler and gets lots of girls. I'd like her to spend the night with him at some point in the story. Maybe after the thrill of seeing him wrestle for the first time?

It would be good to have some other kooky wrestlers around at events - and definitely the threat of other women looking to steal Hunter away from her. Happy to hear ideas you may have too. Thanks – Dave.

It wasn't *every* detail of the story that I'd imagined writing but it was enough to get my ghostwriter started. Hunter and Ella would have a meet-cute followed by an introduction to professional wrestling. Then their relationship would be under strain because of it. Due to the time difference in America he replied at four in the morning. I awoke to a very enthusiastic response. I would soon learn that they are always positive at the start… before you've paid them.

### GHOSTWRITER #1:

Hi Dave, I've reviewed the notes you've supplied. I think there's enough there to fill ten thousand words. For this kind of story, are you looking for a standard PG13 type of drama, or perhaps something more risqué? I have no issues with either option, just curious what you're looking for. Also, regarding an ending, are you looking for something open ended (for possible extension) or closed off? The ending could go either way. Looking forward to your feedback!

### ME:

Risqué is fine. Not erotic/pornographic but sex/sexiness is definitely a part of it. Ella's attracted to him as a topless waiter, other women are also attracted to him as a wrestler. It should be the kind of story where if they were gorillas instead of people, that there is always an alpha male gorilla and the female gorillas all want to mate with him. Does that make sense? I'm open to hearing other endings or suggestions. What did you have in mind for open ended?

### GHOSTWRITER #1:

Hi Dave, Your gorilla example makes sense to me! I'm definitely open to working on this story. It sounds like it would be a kooky romcom, with the right amount of action and sexy time to make it flavorful but classy. The ending could probably do well with a cliffhanger, where Hunter plays the bad guy role in such a way that readers won't know if he leaves or stays, and whether or not he gets the girl. But I'm a stickler for cliffhangers, not everyone is.
In a part 2, for example, both issues could be addressed and come full circle leading to the moral dilemmas that accompany each. I'm currently booked with 3 concurrent projects, but I would be available to start work on this by the 30th/31st,

which is when the 7 day leadtime would begin. Delivery would be expected on or about the 6th of Jan. If that timeline works for you, we can start hashing out a plan for the plot from now, and initiate the gig when it's time. Looking forward to your reply!

### ME:

Okay. Let's say it can be a cliffhanger for now. I'm happy for his character to slowly become less and less perfect as the story goes on. He's a bad boy and she likes him anyway. I'm pleased that you like the concept. I'd like to add that 'Hunter' feels like an alias to me. And that his real name is something more ordinary. It could be a reveal at some point...perhaps when he trusts her a bit more? I will book you for a ten thousand word gig on the 30th. What other plot points would you like to hash out now?

### GHOSTWRITER #1:

Hi Dave, Excellent! I appreciate the opportunity! One key plot point was going to be his real name if you had any ideas for it, so kudos on spotting that one! I'm interested to know what time period you're thinking about. I'm getting strong mid 90s vibes. Also interested to hear what your thoughts about what Ella was doing before she met him (work/relationships/etc) are. I'm getting the impression that they're mid 20s or early 30s. Keep me posted if you have any new input or ideas! I may model Hunter after a cross between Hulk Hogan, Rick Flair, The Undertaker, and Goldberg. Looking forward to this project!

The ghostwriter was keen as mustard. Now...if you are a fan of wrestling like I am you will read the names of those suggested wrestlers and have no idea what kind of character these people would meld into. Hulk Hogan is a tanned, balding, flamboyant, shirt tearing, catchphrase spouting cartoon character. Ric Flair, aka *The Nature Boy*, is known for his catchphrase 'Woooooooo!' and is admittedly also very charismatic despite his old age. The Undertaker is a tall, dark, tattooed, demon-type that attempts to bury his oponents. And finally Goldberg is a bald, intimidating, muscular, brick of a man famous for a winning streak and his 'man of action' attitude. With the exception of Hulk Hogan and Ric Flair, who have some notable overlap, each of these characters is completely different. So as you will see in the exchange below I tried to cut it down for him. I also tried to make the character of Ella easy for him to write by making her a ghostwriter too!

ME:

Ha ha. A young slightly cocky Ric Flair meets Goldberg sounds good. Full of ability and potential - everyone thinks he's going to be a star. I see them as 25-30 years old - definitely. Ella's out of school and has been wanting to write as a full time job. She can't get steady work and so she picks up a lot of re-writing and ghostwriting gigs. That's her dream but day-to-day paying the bills she should have a fairly boring job. An assistant for a lawyer or something? That's why meeting Hunter is exciting and an escape from her routine, She's probably dated on and off but no one serious lately. Her only 'major' relationship was a college one that fizzled out in the real world. Ella's at an age where her friends are starting to settle down. She's always the bridesmaid. Strong 90's vibe huh? I hadn't considered setting it in the 90's but I like that. I'm not fussed on the real name. Whatever you want.

The ghostwriter was already bringing ideas to the table. I hadn't thought of setting it in the 90's but I did genuinely like that idea. That was the *Attitude Era* of professional wrestling and it was the time period when my brother William and I started watching wrestling together. It was a good thing to pitch to me.

And so the ghostwriting gig was arranged. The week of writing time went by and I was delivered 9,823 words.

In the next section of this book the delivery from the ghostwriter will be in regular Times New Roman font while my thoughts about this work are in *italics*. After each paragraph of their writing I will share some feedback and assess how the project is unfolding. I wanted you to experience the work of the ghostwriter in this book as I received it.

This means I haven't changed a single word. Any spelling mistakes or grammatical errors that were made have been left in intentionally. I want to stress that I haven't added or removed anything at all. I have merely critiqued their words in *italics*.

I should add as a general warning that – as we discussed – the story is risqué and shouldn't really be read by minors. This isn't full on erotica but there are adult ideas at play immediately and I'm critiquing this with an adult reader in mind.

Enjoy the beginning of *Dropping the Belt*.

## Chapter 1

Ella found her way back to the dimly lit table where the familiar wooden chair was. All the chairs in the club were wooden, but she'd taken claim to that one. It was the chair she'd seen upon entering, after the hugs and cheek kisses with old friends she'd only met a few times before. Her college roommate Amanda was getting married in a few days. Amanda thought of inviting Ella to the party as a tribute to their time in college. Some of Ella's friends were present as well, but she wasn't there for them. They were huge gossips.

*Dropping the Belt is underway! This is exciting. Okay first of all it seems unlikely that a nightclub would have nothing but wooden chairs. Think about any nightclub you've ever been to. IF there were any chairs at all they would be metal – and welded to the ground. Or lounge like seats. A wooden chair isn't durable and would invite a fight between drunk patrons. Secondly: are they 'old friends' or have they 'only met a few times?' How confusing! So she's invited to the party 'as a tribute' (how very Hunger Games) but NOT the wedding? Does that sound like she's been invited to this gathering but that she won't be attending the wedding? Ella's other nameless friends are there too – but they are gossips. Why is Ella staying friends with them then? That sounds toxic to me.*

The nightclub was decorated special for the occasion. Ella was quite surprised at all of the cock balloons and dick themed paraphernalia laying around. There were straws and napkins adorned with massive hard ones. The sights didn't bother her as much as she'd hoped. Getting turned on was a problem she'd had recently. Her ex didn't quite do it for her. The other guys over the last few months couldn't do it for her either. Their stamina to keep up with her was always the reason. Poor guys.

*Wow. A lot to unpack here…*
*They've booked out the whole nightclub? That seems expensive. So there is just a bunch of penis paraphernalia 'laying around' and not hung up? That's some shoddy decorating if you ask me. Does seeing random penises upset her? No. Ella's not bothered. Although she seems to WANT to be bothered by them! They don't bother her as much as she'd hoped? She HAD hoped that they would bother her SO much that she would get horny. Because as she says – Ella hasn't been horny. Her ex didn't make her horny. The 'parade' of guys (how many is a parade?) haven't made her horny. Reading between the lines every guy has been premature with her. That means either all men in this universe are not good at sex or she's sooooo sexy that they lose control right away. 'Poor guys' indeed!*

The party opened with the standard bridesmaid's games and jokes. Time passed quickly, and since Ella wasn't one of the bridesmaids for this wedding, she found solace in her strawberry daiquiris, watching the male dancers swing themselves at the other ladies. After the first few hours, to her surprise, one of the waiters working the tables caught her eye. The man was beyond fit. His body was a tribute to pure masculinity, the kind every magazine muscle head aspires to have. How had she not seen him before? His salty blonde hair made him stand out from the others.

*I don't love that we breeze past the formality of games and jokes. That would have been a good opportunity to get to know Ella. 'Time passed quickly' is also a lazy way to write. Things happened and time passed. Meh. So, she's not a bridesmaid? No WAY is she going to Amanda's wedding. There are male dancers 'swinging' themselves at the ladies. That sound like they are strippers doesn't it? It's very unclear though. And what a phrase: 'magazine muscle head.'*

*I guess she's been super engrossed with her gossipy friends for a few hours and not looked up. Ella is drinking strawberry daiquiris. Are we to believe that this Adonis who is 'beyond fit' has been bringing her drinks for up to three hours and she hasn't noticed him? I agree! How HAD she not seen him before? I'm a bit worried about the second use of the word 'tribute' here as well.*

The waiter approached her table, and for the first time since arriving, Ella couldn't speak to reorder her drink. The man smiled and took the empty glasses from the table. He winked at her and said he'd be right back. His shirtless body mesmerized her, like a snake charmed with music. The shoulders were powerful, of the kind to lift a woman and hold her up for hours. She found herself daydreaming about getting a massage from this man. His biceps were large, but not cartoonish. They were perfect. His forearms made Ella uncomfortable to think about anything aside from a decent back rub. How was he just a body working at the nightclub?

*Confirmed! He HAS been bringing her drinks all night. He's in shape... we get it. But in what scenario would any man hold a woman up for hours at a time? Why is that appealing? Is it like doing the famous lift from Dirty Dancing but then just holding Ella in the air for hours? How long would it take before you wanted him to put you down? It's funny to me that the first thing she imagines – what with her inability to get horny – is getting a massage from this man. Has she seen lots of other biceps and been like 'Ew...too cartoonish yeah?' Ella's 'uncomfortable to think about anything aside from a decent back rub?' What an ugly sentence that was. And well done Ella! Way to reduce him to 'just a body' right away. Objectification works both ways lady.*

The man came back, greeting Ella with a bright smile. She thought about how perfect his face was, and the way his smile brought joy to her from the inside out. She ordered another daiquiri. When the man turned to put in the order with the bar, she found it to be an opportunity to get handsy. Ella grabbed his wrist, calling out for him to wait. As if she'd forgotten something. The thickness of the man's wrist meant she couldn't wrap her fingers completely around it. That was a promising start. The man apologised and asked if he could help with anything else. Ella released her grip, bumbling over her words for a moment before composing herself.

*Biceps? Perfect. Shoulders? Perfect. And guess what? His FACE is also perfect. For some unknown reason he's come back to the table immediately. Did they call him over? Nah. But since they've booked out the whole nightclub I guess there is nobody else to wait on. Ella found her voice and decided to get 'handsy' with him? So she's gauging the thickness of his wrist. Is that supposed to be a telling sign of penis girth or something? Ella is drunk isn't she? She's been smashing drinks down for hours. Why on Earth is he apologising to her?*

"I wanted to ask you how much the, um," Ella paused and hesitated. "How much a Mai Tai is?"
The shirtless waiter replied "It's open bar, so whatever you like!"
"Oh, right!" Ella said, knowing full well it was open bar. "Silly me!"
"Would you like one?"
"Oh, I think I'll wait until I finish the daiquiri before I try one. Thanks!"
"Word." the waiter said as he began to leave again.
"What's your name?" Ella asked coyly, hoping he would hear her but not knowing if she even spoke the words. Her shyness sometimes got the better of her.

"You can call me Hunter," he said.

"Hunter, got it!" Ella sat back in her chair, proud to have solicited with the waiter. She began plotting how to catch his phone number. The rest of the women at the party were mostly trotting around on the dancefloor or experimenting with the male stripper whose time was expiring soon. The thirsty ladies were seeing how far they could make him go, flashing themselves at him and pulling out cash to be more convincing. The problem was that real strippers weren't as free or playful as you could find in the phonebook. The majority of them are fun to be around and keep the party going, which is what they're paid to do.

*'How much is it?' she asks. Hunter responds: 'whatever you like' – which is not an answer to that question. A better answer would be 'free' because they are. 'Whatever you like' implies that she can pay what she feels like paying. Ella's already GOT a daiquiri by the way. Not that I'm counting her drinks or anything! Usually you would solicit something from a person rather than solicit a person. It's a common phrase for prostitution. Is THAT what the ghostwriter means? And Hunter says 'word' as if that's a cool thing to say. I guess it's the 90's? So maybe he might say that. The other women are 'experimenting' with the male stripper? So they are getting weird with him. It's a dancefloor orgy! Hopefully not Amanda though, right? She's getting married soon. Oddly the gossipy women are making themselves the subject of said gossip. ALSO 'whose time was expiring soon' makes it sound like the stripper has only moments to live! Is he ninety-five years old? What is happening there? The ladies are flashing HIM and then paying him to be more convincing? That's a confusing phrase. Ella sounds knowledgeable about strippers doesn't she? This isn't her first hen's party.*

Hunter arrived back at Ella's table with her daiquiri, and set down a Mai Tai beside it. "I figured I would bring you the Mai Tai, just if you wanted it sooner than later."

"Gee, thanks! Now I have to drink it." Ella joked.

"Only if you like it." Hunter stood by for a moment, observing the crowd. "Your friends are pretty wild, I see. Are you waiting for a dance partner?"

"Oh no, I'm just here to support my old roommate. She's over there." Ella pointed across the room to the table with all the gifts on it and a giant cock balloon hovering over a cake. Amanda was there with a few of her bridesmaids taking pictures on their disposable cameras and laughing at all the cock-themed decor.

"Would you like to dance?"

"I'm not one for dancing…"

Hunter cut her off, "C'mon, let's dance." He gently grabbed her wrist and lifted her by the arm out of the chair.

*She's got a daiquiri and Hunter brought her another one AND a Mai Tai. He says Ella only has to drink it 'if she likes it.' How will she know if she likes it WITHOUT drinking it? I love that they have been there for hours and nobody has cut the cake. Aren't they hungry? Wouldn't they like some food to go with all the free booze? And what kind of bar tab are they running up here? The cake is decorative, like the big old cock balloon hovering over it. The women at the hens are still SO amused by the cock themed décor too. Like there are so many dicks in the room that they are still discovering them. Disposable cameras for the hen's night is a bit random… but anyway. Hunter asks if she needs a dance partner – she says no. Hunter asks her to dance again – she say no. He 'gently grabbed' Ella by the wrist and forced her to dance. Third times a charm! No consent here…*

"At least let me take a sip of the daiquiri, first!" She chugged a few sips before being led to the dance floor. Hunter's bare body was too warm for her not to remain close to him the whole time. His thong exposed much of his thighs and his behind. The shirtless waiter knew how to keep a girl interested. Ella's impunity from being seen with another guy was that she was single. It was okay for her, but the others at the party all had boyfriends or husbands. The gossip, of course, would be about her with the waiter and how free Ella was with him.

The song ended and Ella escorted Hunter back to the table. "Wonderful," she said. "My daiquiri is now spiked, and as soon as I sip it you're going to take me away and have a good 'ol time, huh pal?"

Hunter didn't quite react the way Ella hoped, but he smiled and said "Oh yea!" The man let her chug some of her drink before attempting to head off. Ella set her drink down while still taking huge gulps from it.

*Wow...okay... so first of all he's wearing a THONG? This was not in the brief! Hunter was meant to be a topless waiter not a bottomless one! He's almost naked and still super warm. He's 'keeping a girl interested' by basically being nude? Also we learn here that Ella is the only single girl there. Why would they gossip about her when ALL of them are experimenting with strippers? Is she being 'free' with him really? She danced with him ONCE. He's the one in the THONG. 'Oh my God did you see Ella DANCE with that guy?' says the married woman grinding on a stripper. 'What a slut! She's being so FREE with him!' replies the other gossipy girl as she takes off her bra to flash another stripper. HUH? When they return to the table she implies that her drink might be spiked AND accuses Hunter of doing it. Does he deny it? Nope! He smiles and says 'Oh yea!' So he DID spike it? And he's admitting it? Are you serious? THEN... and this is the MOST crazy bit if you ask me... Ella CHUGS the drink and takes 'huge gulps' from it. Oh my...*

With the icy concoction starting a brain freeze, Ella quickly blurted out "So we should hook up … I mean hang out later." She paused, the alcohol and brain freeze taking over. "I think you seem really nice."

Hunter replied, "It's not really part of my job, you know. I'm here to make sure you ladies have a good time. I don't mean to lead you on or anything."

"No no no, I mean we should go on a date." Ella held her head with both hands, the frosty goodness was taking a toll on her.

"Are you asking me out?" Hunter emphasised himself in that statement. The deejay started playing some loud bass music for the girls on the dancefloor. Of course the good music was saved for them, but Ella was about to score a date with the sexiest waiter of the club. Her friends' activities were not nearly as important as Hunter's attention.

*Ella's wasted now. Her head is so heavy that she has to hold it up with both hands. How dumb is Hunter sounding by the way? She says she wants to 'hook up' then 'hang out' and THEN in plain English states 'we should go on a date.' Hunter's response? 'Are you asking me out?' YES Einstein. Is that how you spell DJ by the way? I always think of 'Deejay' from the video game Streetfighter when I see it written that way. That (and the way he wrote 'yeah' as 'yea' in the last paragraph) really points out to me that English might not be this ghostwriter's first language. He did choose a Caucasian American male profile picture though. Perhaps it's the American Education system that has let him down. And the 'deejay' is playing the 'good' music for the girls on the dancefloor? Ella, I believe you'll find that the music is for everyone! It's not exclusively being played for those girls because it's MUSIC – and sound travels. If you can hear it then it's playing for you too!*

"I don't ask for things, but you are really good at dancing." Ella had to shout.

"Sure!" Hunter said. Ella could only see his lips move.

"It's okay, I understand," Ella said, thinking he said no.

Yelling his response, "No! I said SURE! Yes, let's go on a date!" Hunter wrote his number down on a napkin, and Ella immediately pocketed it. "My phone is my home number. Call me when you want! Let's dance!" Ella downed the last of the daiquiri and drank the entire Mai Tai as if it were just a single shot. Hunter idled by, dancing minimally and shuffling as he stood looking over Ella's shoulder. Her dress was revealing, and he was able to casually catch a glimpse of her from that stance.

*'I don't ask for things but you really are good at dancing.' So if he was BAD at dancing you wouldn't be into him? You wouldn't be asking for 'things' from him? How foreign does the line 'My phone is my home number' sound? And the line: 'call me when you want.' Duh Hunter. That's how phones work! He's standing beside her – sorry 'idling' by like a CAR - dancing 'minimally' as she's having even more alcohol. Then he looks down her dress like a creep. How endearing.*

Ella stood up, immediately feeling the rush of her booze. The night went on and they danced, making a vibrant spectacle for the other girls in the group who only partially cheered them on. A small handful of the girls who were closer friends to Ella than Amanda were not so pleased. They didn't engage the sight. Instead they vied for Amanda's attention, and began listing all the reasons why Ella wasn't a good choice for Hunter. Of the wedded girls, some started recalling how recluse Ella was at their weddings, and how she had the honor of being their bridesmaid. They eventually started listing the reasons why they would be better choices, though they hadn't met Hunter until that night.

Amanda was just proud her old roommate was finally letting loose and getting some fun out of the party. The pair hadn't done much of anything together since graduation. Though, the bride did consider cutting in between Ella and Hunter. Hunter was all muscle, and she liked that.

*They go from no dancing to SO much dancing. And her friends are now 'partially' cheering them on. Why do they care who Ella dances with? ALL of them have boyfriends and husbands anyway! And I LOVE that the ones who are better friends with Ella that are 'not so pleased' about it! What's wrong with Ella that she doesn't deserve happiness? They are so mad that they won't even look at her! Instead of looking at the 'spectacle' of Hunter dancing with her they get in Amanda's ear and start 'listing the reasons' Hunter is bad for Ella! They don't even KNOW him! And then the audacity to add that THEY would be better for Hunter! They hate him don't they? They would rather end their marriages and relationships to be with him than let Ella date him. Ha! How ridiculous. Then Amanda decides she's happy for Ella but still considers cutting in! Because she likes muscles. We're off to a really rocky start with this story. You can tell it was written quickly but I'm laughing so hard that I have tears in my eyes.*

## Chapter 2

Hunter waited patiently outside, hiding a single rose behind his back. The time made the streetlights come on while he waited, despite it still being light out. It was 7:00pm. The polo he wore fit very snugly on him, allowing his pectorals to stretch the shirt so the collar could not be buttoned up. Ella was upstairs in her third-floor apartment, peeking down at Hunter standing near the entrance of the building. The pair had been calling back and forth since the hen's night and planned the date for that night. Some of the calls were cute messages left on the other's answering machine. Ella's conservative dress was much more modest than her dress from the party. The black flowery sundress gave way to her calves, which she liked to show off by wearing high heels. With a spritz of perfume, Ella headed out to greet the man she'd been pursuing since the party. That date was her chance to rebound and show the real hens of the party what she could do. They would certainly have something to gossip about if she didn't invite them to her wedding.

*The first two lines tell you: It's 7pm and the streetlights are on – but it's so convoluted. The funniest part of this is that Ella is dressed to show off her calves. Is he a butt guy or a breast man? Neither! Hunter is all about calves. She wants to show the 'real' hens of the party what she can do. Who are the 'real' hens? Huh? Why do we value these opinions anyway? You know what else? Ella has decided – without going on a single date with Hunter yet – that she will be marrying him. AND that she hasn't decided whether she will be inviting her gossipy friends to their wedding. Why IS she friends with them really? And if none of those women are actually friends with Ella – where are her REAL friends?*

Ella confidently walked out and greeted Hunter with a kiss on the cheek and a hug. He kissed back on her cheek and whispered something in her ear. Ella blushed. Then, Hunter revealed the rose he was hiding, commenting how much of a rose Ella was. She blushed even harder, unable to contain her smile.

The pair took a taxi to her favorite Italian restaurant near the downtown area. On the way, they giggled and shared stories. The old cab driver observed their behavior in his mirror, smiling to himself at how coy they were. They were a young pair, obviously lusting for each other. The cabbie didn't want to interfere.

*Hunter whispered something in her ear – but it was just for Ella to hear – NOT for the reader of this story! It's like the end of the film Lost in Translation. Gawd. It made her blush – so it's something sexy, right? 'Uh…I got you this rose…cos YOU are like a rose…' he says as she turns REDDER - proving he's right! I love how the writer doesn't tell us any of the jokes OR stories they shared in the taxi. Maybe hearing them here would help us get to know either character better. Maybe as the reader we would enjoy a joke or a story… Nevermind…*

Hunter paid the cab fare, and they entered the restaurant. He called ahead to make sure they would have a table ready by 8:00pm. They were about a half hour early for the reservation. The restaurant was a popular hot spot for new couples to have their first dates or anniversary dates. It was quite difficult to get a spot there. While getting drinks at the bar, Ella commented on his ability to get things that he wants. "I don't know how you did it, but thanks for booking a table here. I could never get a reservation here if my life depended on it."

"I have my way of convincing people to give me what I want." Hunter said.

"Well then," Ella said, poised for a smart response. "I think you'll need to work a bit harder. I'm not convinced." She was obviously convinced from the moment she saw him, and Ella knew her own feelings as well.

*I'm so glad we are getting a timeline on this! Is it actually important? Hunter has a reservation but they are still there half an hour early? Why? He seems worried about this, as it's 'quite difficult to get a spot there.' Ella thanks him for getting a table while they are at the bar. He hasn't got the table yet and frankly I'm not sure I believe he even HAS a booking. How full on is his reply? He 'has his way' of getting what he wants. She's ready to give it up too! But Ella is trying to be playful and hard to get.*

"I think you'll find that I'm not the kind of guy who backs down from any challenge."
"Oh really? Mr. Man. You wouldn't back down from a challenge even if it was something you knew you couldn't do?" Ella was trying to set him up for a logical trap that would benefit her.
"There's nothing I can't do. I'm the best Goddamned wrestler this city has ever seen, and I will not be hunted. I am The Hunter. And I'm coming for you, next!" Hunter announced as though he were performing a bit. He sat proud and looked off into the wall behind the bar, popping his collar.

*What on Earth was the 'logical trap' that Ella was setting him up for? Was she going to propose some kind of challenge that she knew he couldn't do – in order to win...somehow? There is the big reveal. It's a super weird way to tell Ella that he's a professional wrestler. His way of saying that he's 'The Hunter' sounds mildly threatening too. 'I'm coming for you next' sounds villainous.*

*It's certainly not the way I would have written it. How did his being a professional wrestler never come up in all the phone calls and answering machine messages they shared? And Hunter's big claim is that he's only the best in the CITY. He's not the best in the world? At least he's realistic about it I suppose. He pops the collar of his polo and looks 'off into the wall' behind her. INTO the wall.*

"What was that?" Ella giggled. "Are you really a wrestler?"
Hunter stopped pretending and looked back at Ella, into her eyes. "Oh, yea. That was my line. It's a thing every wrestler has to intimidate their opponents. What did you think?"
Ella let out a scoff, looking down at her drink. His eyes were beautiful but intimidating. "I think it's alright if you're selling cars. But wrestling? C'mon." She paused, looking back at Hunter with a slight grin. "I've written better taglines for insurance commercials than that. But you. You're a wrestler?"

*Is Ella saying she writes taglines for insurance commercials? Is that meant to be her day job? In our early discussion I had asked for her to be a writer… so I suppose that he's taken creative licence here and given her a writing job. She's still not convinced he's a wrestler either. It's a weird thing to lie about Ella…*

"Yea. And I have a match tomorrow night. I wanted to ask you if we could make that a date or something?" He hadn't stopped looking into her eyes.
"Everyone knows that's just an act…"
Hunter cut her off. "No! It's definitely not." Hunter looked away behind the bar again. "We're out there working our asses off to make ends meet. It's tough work! The matches are real. There is some showmanship, like my tagline and maybe the exaggerated injuries, but I guaran-damn-tee you the matches are real."

"Okay hot stuff, I believe you. Wrestling is real." She winked at the end, just as Hunter looked back at her. She wrapped her arm under his and clasped his hand for reassurance.

"It's real. Where's our table, I'm ready to eat." Hunter was ready to eat, but he was also ready to stop the discussion about wrestling. Ella assumed the submissive role.

*Two dates in two nights. I get what he means. He wants Ella to see him in action. But he's staring at her! You can break eye contact any time Hunter! Alright...in all seriousness...DOES Hunter know how professional wrestling works? He's pretty adamant that wrestling is real. She's like 'sure it's real \*wink\*' and Hunter's annoyed! He's defensive. 'It's real!' he says and he's done talking about it. Um... you brought it up Hunter! And it's not real – it's staged. For those readers who are not aware: professional wrestling has a pre-determined outcome and is not 'real' in the same way boxing or UFC is real. The wrestlers are not trying to hurt eachother and win so much as entertain the crowd with story and spectacle.*

The two got their table and ordered food. Drinks and a few plates later, they ordered and shared a chocolate brownie dessert. Hunter offered to pay the bill, but Ella thought they should split it. They began discussing a man's role in a relationship and how paternalistic the world is. Ella sided with the more dominant movement for women, citing how she could write a script for something and be offered less money than a guy who wrote a worse script for the same job. Hunter valued the more traditional views about relationships, however. He wanted to show chivalry and be a gentleman, taking on the role of a classic prince or nobleman. Ella liked the idea of being pampered, but wanted to be sure Hunter knew she was self-sufficient. They laughed about it and moved on, letting the romance of the evening sweep them away.

*Do you know what would be interesting to know about her favourite restaurant? ANYTHING. We zip past the whole meal. Did they eat in silence? They may as well have. Ella is writing screenplays too apparently, but getting paid less than men who write 'worse scripts' for the same job. This whole paragraph is written without a single word from either character. The ideas that they discuss are so big and they are all glossed over here. He wants to take on the role of a 'classic prince or nobleman'? What YEAR is it? It's supposed to be the 90's. The romance of the evening is sweeping them away? Is it romantic? Goodness knows. I can't tell.*

The rest of the night was spent walking around the downtown area, people watching. Hunter was a familiar face to the few people who recognised him. Ella noticed a few of the women who saw Hunter as well, glaring at them with an evil stare as they passed by.

They continued their talks and laughed at many jokes together. Their bond strengthened. Ella remembered that Hunter asked her to watch him wrestle. Feeling a bit sorry for accusing him of being a fake, she told him she'd watch him wrestle. She would be there the next night to watch and cheer him on. Hunter instantly felt a relief inside, letting his comfort with Ella broaden. Despite the earlier conversation, his feelings for Ella had expanded tenfold. That she would watch him wrestle made his anxiety go away. He would have an audience he knew instead of an audience he didn't.

*Hunter is a really familiar face in the downtown area. He was recognised by a 'few' people. What a celebrity! And it sounds like the girls didn't recognise him from wrestling. He's a muscular and allegedly perfect man in a tight polo. They were just checking him out. I'm glad they laughed at 'many' jokes. He sounds SO funny doesn't he? How very lazy to write 'their bond strengthened' too. Wow...*

*Why don't you SHOW us how they bonded instead of just telling us that it did? And because Ella says she will watch and cheer him on his feelings 'expanded tenfold' did they? He must have not really cared at all to start with! Did he have anxiety? Hunter seems like a pretty confident guy, you know, the kind of guy who would wear a THONG all night. He feels better knowing the audience instead of them being strangers? Ha! Can you imagine him filling the arena with people he knows so he feels better about wrestling? Or imagine Hunter trying to meet as many patrons as possible beforehand so he sees more familiar faces as he wrestles.*

Date night ended, and Hunter found himself standing outside of Ella's apartment building. The taxi was waiting at the curb, door open, for Hunter to return. Ella had just gone in after a hug and another kiss on the cheek. The two were playing it rather slow. Ella was testing herself not to be too open with a new guy. Her past relationships always went so fast. They would end just as fast, so she wanted to make sure this one was just right. The cab driver tooted his horn to let Hunter know he was still there.

After getting in and closing the door, Hunter commented to the cab driver, "She's really something special, pops. I don't want to fuck it up."

The old cabbie puts the car in gear and starts driving. "Just treat her right. If she's a good gal and you're a good guy, it'll work out. Just don't hurt her."

"Yea, I know. She's so hot. I just want that every night when I come home, or while I'm working. I can't stop looking at her." Hunter relaxes in his seat.

"She's a very attractive young lady. If she's smart, she'll see past your flaws." The cabbie turns left at an intersection with a blinking yellow light.

"Thanks, pops. I'm headed over to 9th, if you don't mind."

"Sure thing, kid."

They are definitely playing it slow considering the hot and heavy way they danced. Isn't it weird that we skipped over the moment they said goodnight to each other? You'd think that it would be a moment we would enjoy considering this is meant to be a romantic story. Ella wanted to make sure 'this one was just right' like a bowl of porridge! The cab driver has to TOOT his horn at Hunter! How long was he just waiting there? Hunter says goodnight to Ella and then does he just stand there for several minutes? Certainly for long enough to warrant a horn honking. Also, Hunter doesn't live there so the cab driver would still have the meter running, right? He's still going to drop Hunter off. So why does he care if he sits there for a few more minutes? He's getting paid for his time. Hunter calls the cab driver 'pops' – is this because he's a charming old timer or because this taxi driver is actually Hunter's father? And how threatening for him to say 'don't hurt her.' How does Hunter reply to this wise old cab driver? 'She's so hot' he states. And then he says he wants 'that' every night! Ha ha! And he wants it 'while he's working' too! THEN...oh my GOSH... the cabbie says if she's SMART – and that's mildly insulting for Ella - she'll see past your flaws! He's saying Hunter DEFINITELY has flaws AND that she'd be stupid to focus on them! He knows that Hunter is flawed having JUST MET HIM! He really is a wise old cabbie.

## Chapter 3

The venue held about 5000 people. Ella spoke to Hunter that afternoon to say hi and to figure out how she would view his match. The venue would let in guests for free if they knew anyone working there. Ella had to meet someone named Gunther around the side of the building, Hunter advised her. He said Ella's name would be on Gunther's list of VIPs.

When she got in, Ella was led around the venue and given a brief tour of the facility. The wrestling organization had taken full charge of the backstage area, converting it into a full on gym with mirrors and body oil everywhere. Many of the men there were greased up muscles just working out. Ella felt a pang inside. She was definitely turned on. The lack of sex recently made her desires come on stronger than she was used to.

*A 5000 seat venue is massive. AND they'll just let in ANYONE that remotely knows someone that works there? What an awful business model. They mention Gunther a bunch only to NEVER have him appear. So what's the point of him? Some faceless person has time to give her a tour? And why have they set up an entire gym? Ella gets turned on by the men working out. It's not even Hunter working out...*

Hunter came out of his greenroom to greet Ella. They hugged, and the guys around all started teasing. "C'mon guys, this is her first time seeing me work. At least say hi first." Hunter said. Ella shyly waved at them.
All in unison, "Hi first!" The group all laughed and started talking amongst themselves. Ella laughed.
"Sorry about them, we're like a big family here." Hunter said. "Whenever one of us brings a girl to a match we have to make a scene."

"Oh, it's alright! Cool beans." Ella was certainly awkward now that she could expect to be the point of any jokes about Hunter.

"I'm glad you came! You're going to get the phatest seat in the house. I'm on in 30 so until then we usually just workout and grub. Are you hungry? There's a craft table." Hunter spoke fast and seemed highly excitable.

"Um, sure? I didn't know what to expect so I ate a little before I got here." Ella lied.

"Oh, okay. Well there's a ton of snacks over there," Hunter pointed, "and the craft table is over there." Hunter pointed elsewhere. "If you're looking for drinks, you can find them at both tables."

*Hunter has his own greenroom. And how corny are all of the wrestlers calling her 'first'? I appreciate the ghostwriter's attempt at humour though. I'd rather that than 'They told some jokes.' Ella loses all of her edge when she says 'cool beans' and you can immediately tell this was written by a man. She expects to be the 'point' of any jokes – I think it's meant to be the 'butt' of any jokes. More nonsense. Ella's going to get the 'phatest' seat in the house. Was that even a phrase people were saying in the 90's? I don't think so...*

*Hunter is suggesting that in the thirty minutes before they get in the ring and wrestle that they eat a bunch of food and then workout? If you aren't supposed to eat before swimming then you shouldn't eat right before wrestling either! They are going to be sick in the ring if they eat a bunch of 'grub.' And why the workout at all? If you don't have it by now you won't be able to get it in the thirty minutes before you're on. Aren't you just going to make yourself sore or tired? That seems like another bad idea. The geography is wacky too. The craft table is, for some reason, placed away from the snack table? Why? But they have drinks at both tables? Who set that up? Is there someone that's in charge here?*

"Awesome. So what do we do now?" Ella stood, confused about what Hunter's next move was.

"Well, you get to watch me work. I need to start lifting."

"Oh, okay." She hid her emotions, but Ella was excited to see how much he could lift. "I'm going to grab a water and then be right back."

"You know where to go, right?" Hunter idled.

"It's all good."

"Rad. I'll be here." Hunter walked over to the bench press and practically rolled over it backwards before landing on it in one motion. Clearly, he had done that before, but Ella wondered if he was showing off or if that was a normal thing guys did when they worked out.

She walked over to the catering tables, finding them half empty already. The crew and the wrestlers must have already been through them. She found a bottle of water and looked around the area. Besides the gym equipment, and a few stage pieces, the back of the venue was rather boring. Black walls and black ceilings made the area very plain. The lighting was dim, but bright enough to get around. Outside, in the main arena, Ella could hear the crowd oh and awe at the match going on.

*He needs to start lifting? What a great date this is turning out to be! At least Ella acknowledges that it's boring. 'Hey babe come to the gym and watch me workout. There will be a table with snacks for you.' She wants to know how much he can lift. Like Hunter is going to be trying for a personal best here and now! He shouldn't be pushing himself before a match like that! And he's definitely showing off. I'm not sure why they would paint a ceiling black. It would feel too claustrophobic if you ask me. In my mind when she saw him wrestling for the first time I thought it would be from the point of view of an audience member. This feels less impressive.*

*She can hear the crowd and I feel kind of sorry for her as she's missing the show. Ella obviously hasn't seen wrestling before. Wouldn't it make sense to give her the whole experience of the event? She won't be able to compare Hunter to the other wrestlers and know if he's any good. Come and visit him backstage afterwards. In my version I thought Ella would go to a show with some girlfriends and then be surprised to see Hunter. It would have served as a bigger reveal than this.*

Walking back to the workout area, Ella crossed paths with another wrestler. He was wearing a pink fur jacket of a type she'd never seen before. It was very brightly colored, and shouted at her to stop looking at it. The man was almost a foot taller than her. Ella was not short, but no one was a foot taller than her. She looked down, noticing his thick boots which gave him at least four inches of extra height.

"So you're that girl Hunter was talking about. Nice of you to stop by. I hope you don't mind when I beat his ass to the ground later," the intense wrestler said.

"Um, hi? And I don't know much about wrestling, but if Hunter doesn't want to lose, he's not." Ella wasn't afraid of the guy, but she certainly didn't like the way he approached her in conversation.

*Is Ella not familiar with fur? Or jackets? Or does that mean she has never seen a pink fur jacket specifically? The jacket 'spoke' to her? It probably shouted 'Stop looking at me!' Ella knows NOTHING about wrestling but has already decided Hunter can beat this guy even though he's taller than her and presumably Hunter. Also: WRESTLING IS FAKE! The outcome has already been decided! I get that they are staying 'in character' but does this guy need to? If Hunter 'doesn't want to lose, he's not' is badly worded too. Who speaks that way?*

The wrestler laughed. "He's as much of a buzz kill as the rest of 'em. You see this?" He looks down and bolsters the belt he's wearing. "This means I'm the champ, and I don't drop my belt for no one."

"Well, good luck with that, Champ." Ella smiled a fake smile and walked away.

"Tell that kitten he's the weakest runt of the litter." The pink fur wearing wrestler said. Ella didn't acknowledge his statement and kept walking.

The time passed quickly, and Ella was highly aroused watching Hunter workout. His strong shoulders and chiseled abs were working for her. Watching him grunt as she stood by was really, really working for her. She had to turn away a few times to keep from blushing. Surely, she had moistened herself and there was no way to relieve the tension she was feeling.

*He's a 'buzzkill'? I don't think Hunter is a buzzkill! As in: he ruins the party? He doesn't 'drop his belt' for anyone? That's not really the way that phrase works either! 'Dropping the belt' actually means losing your title intentionally. If one wrestler loses he 'drops the belt' to the winner. So this wrestler actually believes that he won't intentionally lose. Imagine her delivering that message. 'Hey Hunter, that guy with the belt that I guess you're fighting tonight told me to tell you that he thinks you are a kitten...and that you are the runt of the litter.' And then 'the time passed quickly' – which as I stated is a lazy way to pass time in a story – but there is probably only twenty minutes until his match. Just enough time for Ella to get all turned on watching Hunter work out, right? She likes his grunting. And WOW. She's wet? Too much information. It's hard to imagine this girl has ever had trouble getting turned on as she has been claiming. Ella seems to be turned on by everything! I don't love the use of the word 'moistened' here either. A lot of people are going to struggle with that sentence. I'm sorry in advance dear reader!*

Hunter stopped working out, and advised Ella he would be starting his match soon. One of the crewmembers came and escorted her to a seat right behind the announcers. It was a prime viewing position for anyone wishing to see the match up close. As the event unfolded, the pink fur wearing wrestler was announced. His name was Buster. When Ella heard his name announced she giggled uncontrollably. The super mean man she met backstage had a weak name and wore pink. This fact reinforced her notion that wrestling was fake.

Buster skipped out to the stage from behind the entrance, wooing the crowd as he made his fashionable entrance to the ring. He was met with a mixture of both boos and cheers. Clearly, he was not very liked by the followers of the show. His speech, front and center to the crowd, was worse than anything Ella had ever written and thrown away. How did these guys get their inspiration, she wondered. When Buster claimed Hunter was after his belt, and the mixed applause shocked Ella.

*Ella gets seated right behind the announcers? That's unusual. I get that the name Buster is pretty lame. He does seem to be all over the place character wise. What is his deal? Did he actually have a skipping rope as he 'skipped out' to the ring? Buster gets booed AND cheered which is rare in wrestling. You're usually a face (good guy) or a heel (bad guy) and that gets defined pretty early on through performance and actions. The crowd KNOWS Buster as he's the current Champion. He's carrying the brand on his shoulders! They should know whether they like him by now and be unified in their response. Cheer OR Boo. Ella interprets this reaction to mean he's not well liked. She gives herself a pat on the back as a writer here stating that she's thrown away better speeches than Buster's best work. The last line is BARELY a sentence. It's hard to re-read. What a mess... Is it too soon to apologise to you again?*

The crowd really seemed to like Hunter. His entrance was quite the theatrics as well. His introduction sounded like something right out of an animal documentary. "The Hunter stalks his prey," and "he's coming for you next." Ella was impressed. Hunter crouched down and stealthily made his way to the ring. The crowd really loved his tactics. He received way more cheers than Buster.

After entering the ring and squaring up with the pink fur man, Ella noticed his cheetah leggings for the first time. "How silly," she said aloud before laughing. He was shirtless again, and this time she could clearly see his well-defined back muscles. Falling into the crowd's preference for Hunter, Ella felt quite at ease with the environment. Despite her ideas that wrestling was fake, Ella truly felt as if this was a fitting lifestyle for Hunter.

The matched progressed, and after the two men slammed each other a few times, they became quite sweaty, but only Buster appeared fatigued. Ella noticed how Hunter was certainly working up a sweat but maintained his composure.

*'Quite the theatrics' indeed! What bad grammar! He means 'nature documentary' (not animal documentary) but I get it. The crowd are losing their minds at how well he can 'crouch down' and make his way to the ring. Wait until they actually get to see him wrestle! 'If his crouching tactics are THIS good...well!' Why does Ella refer to Buster as 'the pink fur man' when she KNOWS his name? She thinks his leggings are silly? So much so that she says it out loud. I imagine the ring announcer turning around at her comment. Hunter was 'shirtless again' which confuses me. Was he wearing a shirt as he worked out? I wouldn't have thought so. Ella also decides that this is 'a fitting lifestyle for Hunter' which feels kind of judgmental to say. 'This is fine for HIM...but not for me.' I think that we are meant to tie that last line to the fact that Hunter has stamina, which is very important to Ella as none of her exes had it. He's sweaty but composed. Every girl's fantasy!*

Hunter kept reminding himself to breathe in and out slowly. His composure was part of the character. His ice cold expression was meant to strike fear into his opponents while simultaneously keeping a distant and silent attack at the ready. As the match came to a close, Hunter attempted a body slam from the corner of the ring. Buster was on his hands and knees when Hunter hit. The motion caused Buster to flatten out. Then, Hunter attempted a hold to win the match. Buster, to the surprise of everyone, broke the hold and managed to flip Hunter on his stomach, gaining the advantage. Holding Hunter's arm at his chest, Buster kept a knee to the back of Hunter's neck, forcing a tap out from him.

*How long has Hunter been doing wrestling professionally that he has to keep reminding himself to breathe? It's not second nature yet? Also this description makes his character seem like a distant silent type, yet at the restaurant he was jovial and talkative giving the impression that his wrestling persona was chatty and cocky. He was claiming to be the best in the city and so forth. This version of The Hunter seems stoic with his 'cold expression.' And Hunter loses to Buster. Since wrestling is choreographed ahead of time Hunter would have known this result. So he invited Ella on a date to the wrestling to watch him lose?*

The booing of the crowd meant they weren't happy with Hunter's performance, but also that Buster was able to keep his belt. Knowing the belt was just a symbol and not a real championship belt, Ella was able to reconcile the loss. Hunter, on the other hand, really wanted to beat Buster without going through the politics of the management. He lay, motionless on the ring floor, until the crowd started their departure. This worried Ella. She thought he'd been knocked unconscious somehow. Once the majority of the crowd was up and making their way to the exits, the referee kneeled down next to him and helped him up.

He was holding his hand to his abs when he finally saw Ella sitting behind the announcers. She waved and he smiled at her, winking as he did so.

*They are booing Buster – not Hunter. They are booing the outcome – not his performance within the match. The belt is just a symbol? This isn't Batman. It is a 'real' championship belt in the universe they are playing in. It still has value and lets people know who the best wrestler is! But Ella dismisses it based on the fact that wrestling is fake – so the belt is meaningless. Hunter wanted to ACTUALLY beat Buster and win the belt? Without 'going through the politics' of the management? So like... he was going to sneak a win and therefore be the champion without management having a say? And why is Hunter lying motionless? He was forced to tap out – he wasn't knocked unconscious! He should still have the ability to move. Why does Ella worry that he's been knocked out? He wasn't! She watched the match didn't she? Does Ella think she's been so distracted and giggly that she's missed a knock out punch?*

Ella was escorted backstage by one of the crew members. Upon entering the makeshift gym area, she saw Buster and Hunter sharing a beer. They were all smiles, rubbing shoulders and laughing.
"I thought you had me after that drop, man. That was a good one." Buster said.
"Oh, dude, I thought so too. But you did that high school move on me again! I didn't even remember that was possible." Hunter tipped his beer at Buster. "There she is! Ella, come meet the rest of the dudes!"
The greetings were highly informal, and Ella became more relaxed with them as she was introduced. Jokes were made, and even Ella took a few jabs at Hunter. They all laughed about it and spoke highly of Hunter.

*Yet another faceless crew member leads her around. The wrestlers are 'rubbing shoulders' together? Okay... so the way they chat to one another is as though neither one had any idea how that match would pan out. Both seem surprised and amazed by the outcome. That's not what wrestling IS though. It's carefully planned out like a dance. Sometimes professional wrestlers improvise in the ring but the result is always determined beforehand. And 'you did that high school move on me again' is such a weird phrase. Did they attend the same high school? Does it mean that the move is a basic one you might learn at a high school wrestling level? I'm lost... At least they all spoke highly of Hunter in front of Ella.*

## Chapter 4

A few phone calls, and several dates later, Ella found herself sitting behind the announcers again, watching Hunter. This time, he was wrestling another flamboyant guy named Kong. The large black man with tribal facial scarring was incredibly scary. He was not the kind of person Ella would want to meet randomly in public. The truth was, Kong was a polite and giving guy. He kept his relationship with another wrestler a secret, but everyone had their suspicions. Ella knew immediately that he was hiding his true self.

After Hunter pinned Kong and won the match, they met up back stage for beer. During one of the exchanges, Kong suggested Ella be Hunter's valet. After a bit of explaining, Hunter didn't know if it would be a good idea or not. He and Ella were close, having developed their relationship quite far in the past few weeks. They hadn't been intimate yet, which the other wrestlers didn't believe.

*Time passes…time passes… lazily. Every other wrestler is flamboyant. Isn't Hunter the more outgoing? He's the thong-wearing waiter putting himself out there. The description of Kong feels sort of borderline racist to me. He's black and scary and not 'the kind of person' Ella would want to meet in the real world. That makes her seem sort of racist doesn't it? Ella knew 'immediately' that he was hiding his true self? It doesn't sound like it! It reads like Ella judged him as a scary man and then later learned that he might be gay. Although it doesn't say he was in a relationship with another MALE wrestler it feels implied by the way he is hiding it. If they are 'like a family' as described by Hunter then shouldn't he feel comfortable enough to tell them all? Kong suggests Ella become a valet for Hunter and accompany him to the ring. Hunter doesn't like the idea. And here we learn that they haven't been intimate yet. They are still taking it slow I guess!*

Hunter didn't think it would hurt anything to try it out, but wanted Ella to be the decision-maker. At that time, Hunter did not have a manager. The three of them talked it over and began to develop a storyline for how Ella came to be, and why she wasn't there in the beginning. Hunter needed to be tamed, and that was their story. He had been lost, wandering around, only to be captured again by Ella. She needed a name, however. It took her a while to conceptualize what she was getting into, but Ella called up Hunter once she had it. They would go into the ring at the next match as Hunter and Obsession. Seeing this as a job opportunity, Ella stopped working for the ad agency she was at. While she liked writing up short snippets and things, the world of wrestling really came crashing down on her. Meeting Hunter was probably one of the best things that's happened to her since she graduated college. So much so, in fact, that her contacts from the party weren't even important to her anymore.

*Okay... so she WANTS to be his valet? From everything we know about Ella she is shy and likes to blush. So why on Earth would she want to do this? Some dialogue would have been helpful to explain her interest! Also The Hunter character needed to be tamed? He was too wild? We haven't seen anything to suggest how he's wild and untamed. He seems 'silent and deadly' if anything. Ella comes up with the name and character of Obsession. Is she obsessed with Hunter? Is that where the inspiration comes from? So we finally get to find out what her day job is. Ella works at an advertising agency. Well that's good to know...oh wait...she just QUIT her job? Ella saw THIS as a job opportunity and QUIT her job to be his VALET? In my original email I had her filling in as his valet so she would experience the reactions of the crowd but I NEVER imagined her quitting her job. Ella quits BEFORE she's even done it too! She doesn't know if she likes it yet! ALSO Ella was so high and mighty about her writing before this. She's thrown that job away!*

*What if she and Hunter break up? Geez! HAS the world of wrestling really come 'crashing down' on Ella? That definitely hasn't come across! Meeting Hunter has been NICE but I'm not sure it's been the BEST thing for her. I mean... how much IS Hunter getting paid? He's still taking side jobs as a shirtless waiter to make ends meet. And he does the actual wrestling - Ella's only going to valet. So she's definitely not going to be making as much as Hunter. Quitting her job seems insane to me! Her 'friends' from the party have been reduced to 'contacts' now? What? So I guess if she married Hunter then none of them would be invited! This paragraph is a turning point in this story. The ghostwriter has definitely made some interesting decisions here. They don't seem to fit with the characters... but I guess we should give him the benefit of the doubt? He knows what he's doing, right?*

She loved the environment around wrestling so much more. The gossip of her former friends was meaningless compared to the stories and events her newfound friends had. She was Obsession, and he was Hunter. He was not hunted, or haunted, but he needed Obsession to win. Ella thought herself quite cleaver to come up with that one.
The crowd received her quite well during the next match. In fact, and she didn't know if it was her costume or not, the crowd cheered harder then they'd ever cheered before. At least, for Ella, it seemed that way. With Obsession, Hunter could win a title. It sold tickets. Hunter hoped to win against Buster in a rematch for the belt. Ella was going to help make that happen.
Though, for Ella, being out by the ring gave her a clearer idea of who Hunter's audience really was. A mixture of the core fans was always met with a variety of women. Ella was perpetually faced with their screams and professions of love for Hunter. It was somewhat demotivating, yet empowering.

*Yes... the word 'cleaver' is wrong. Ella's in love with wrestling now? That has not come across at all. She's been giggling and mocking it! She has become FRIENDS with the other wrestlers? Really? Okay... sooooo... he was 'not hunted or haunted'? What are you TALKING about? DOES he need her to win? The crowd LOVES her. Loudest cheering ever! But it sounds like she attributes it to her (probably sexy) costume. How annoying that Ella thinks Hunter can't win a title without her. She saw him fight once! She's so high and mighty isn't she? Ella thinks that her accompanying Hunter to the ring is selling more tickets than usual too. What an ego! But then she's so insecure about the other women that yell out to Hunter. She finds it 'demotivating yet empowering' too. That makes zero sense.*

During one match, Hunter became angry. His comeback from losing was welcomed, but the stunned Obsession rooted for Hunter anyway. The anger caused him to do a few things he wouldn't have done otherwise, but he won the match because of it. Ella saw that as a positive. When the referee called the match, the crowd instantly started chanting "Heel! Heel! Heel!" over and over again. Not knowing what to do, Ella just kept her composure and led Hunter backstage.
"Why are they saying heel? I don't understand." Ella asked.
"I was mad, Ella. The moves I made and the way I was acting took points away from my good guy routine. It's nothing to worry about – it happens sometimes."
"Oh, so it's like a thing? It doesn't mean that you should heel for me, right?"
"No, no. Nothing like that! C'mon. Let's get a beer."

*This is so badly written. Ella was stunned by his anger but decided to 'root for him' anyway? You're HIS valet. That's your only job! He's angry and his 'comeback from losing' was welcomed? As in...he's been a big loser up to this point? Again – this writing is hard to read – but she's saying he's been a loser.*

*No wonder Hunter's mad about it! At least he got the win. It's so odd the way he describes losing 'good guy' points. Like the crowd is keeping track on some kind of scorecard. Ella still doesn't know much about wrestling. Good thing she didn't quit her job...oh...never mind. Why would he 'heel' for her? What nonsense.*

The pair relax and get settled in. Ella remembers that it has been one month since they started dating and reminds Hunter. They express their gratitude for one another and have a few laughs. They realize what they've accomplished together in the last month, and reminisce about it.

"I still can't believe I left my secure job at the ad agency to be a valet. When the girls hear about this, they'll freak!" Ella laughed.

"I'm just glad we can spend time together, whether in the ring or outside of it. I like having you around." Hunter wanted to be the first one to say 'I love you' but he couldn't bring himself to do it in that moment.

Ella picked up on his insecurity. "I'm glad we are together all the time too. It makes me feel like we're meant to be together. I've never met a guy like you before."

"I've never met a girl like you before either. And I've met a lot of girls." Hunter realized his statement was rude, but didn't have enough time to recover.

"I'm sure you've met a lot of girls, but now I'm the only girl you'll ever need." Ella shot back.

"Exactly! That's why we're perfect for each other. I..." Hunter couldn't bring himself to say it again. Something was holding him back.

*I can't focus on the spelling errors...there are too many to keep track of! They have only been dating for ONE MONTH! And she quit her job? THIRTY DAYS. The ghostwriter keeps writing 'they make some jokes' and 'they have some laughs'* as if that means anything at all. It's not funny to write 'Hunter says the funniest thing ever' because we don't know what that funny thing is! It's poorly written. Ella says the only thing that makes sense. WE can't believe you left your SECURE job either! And now the validation of the 'girls' IS important again? A minute ago it didn't matter! Hunter loves her but he can't bring himself to say it. He's saying he's 'met a lot of girls' to her? This is Hunter bragging. This feels like a bigger conversation. Maybe one to have before you QUIT YOUR JOB for a guy Ella!

On a whim, and in an attempt to recover from his insulting statement, Hunter suggests Ella spend the night at his place. She obliges, but reminds Hunter that they'll be traveling the next day for their next match. Ella also comments that the amount of traveling their doing is taking a toll on her. She's feeling the fatigue of their adventures together. In the taxi on the way to Ella's apartment, the pair talk about it.

"The time spent in the car is really more time than we spend at the arenas, if you think about it." Ella said.

"No, I know. There were times when I would show up, change, wrestle, and then drive back home, only to have to work at the bar for a full shift. It was crazy." Hunter said.

"I mean, I wouldn't mind spending the night. It makes more sense than just meeting up tomorrow morning. Can we stop by my place so I can make a bag first?" Ella asked.

"Of course. Makes sense to me. But don't take too long."

*Ella is going to spend the night! In my brief I assumed this would be after seeing him wrestle. Now, seemingly the first time she's spending the night, is punctuated by the fact that they have to work the next day. So that's not romantic is it?*

*Also to suggest it 'on a whim' and to recover from his 'insulting statement' is SO sexy isn't it? Also we learn that the amount of travelling is taking a toll on her? That might be the case if she was STILL working. Ella's not burning the candle at both ends. Also she's NOT actually wrestling! She's not exerting herself the way Hunter is. Does she have chronic fatigue or something? It sounds like he's not making enough money doesn't it? He still has to drive back and work a full shift at the bar. It sounds like Hunter is the tired one! But by all means keep complaining to him about how tired YOU are Ella! Sure we can swing by your place to pack a bag – just be quick about it! How rude. This feels like it's too much work doesn't it? Relationships should be fun at the start. If you are both exhausted and snapping at eachother after only one month you should take a step back and think it over.*

"What?" Ella's heart sank. Another command and insult from Hunter, she thought.
"I said sure. But don't take too long."
"I heard what you said, but I don't know why you said that? You've never asked me to hurry up before." Ella was one phrase away from flipping over to her Obsession persona. The savage beast woman who commands Hunter around was about to become her real personality.
"Oh, I'm not saying hurry up. I meant that I wouldn't want to hold a cab for too long. Unless we should get another cab?" Hunter realized he was being mean. His stage persona was turning heel, but Ella didn't know or recognize it yet.
"I hope that's what you meant." The Obsession personality came out anyway, but only slightly. The cab stopped by her place, where she grabbed the bag she had already prepared. She was in and out of the apartment in under five minutes.
"That was damn fast! Did you get everything you needed?" Hunter wasn't sure how to approach the situation.

*ANOTHER command and insult? I'm not sure he's been commanding her so far. In fact, Hunter let Ella decide whether or not to be his valet. How can it be ANOTHER command if – as she says – 'you've never asked me to hurry up before.' This sounds like the first command he's made. Her character is now a SAVAGE BEAST WOMAN? So the only one who can 'tame' The Hunter is a savage? Huh? How can a presumably untamed savage tame someone else? And her character 'commands' Hunter around? So Obsession tamed him by bossing him around? How quickly does Hunter flip the script? 'Oh I'm not saying hurry up!' Except that's what 'don't take too long' means doesn't it? Ella had already prepared a bag? Was she always planning on a sleepover and just waiting for Hunter to suggest it? So she hurries and he doesn't know HOW to handle it.*

"Yep, all set. Everything's in the bag." She laughed, "In the bag, get it?"
Hunter laughed loudly. "Oh yea, I'm down. I love …" he hesitated. He wanted to say 'your jokes' but realized his opportunity. "I love you."
Ella paused, and blushed. "Tsk. I love you too, babe." They kiss, touching lips briefly, before she quickly breaks the kiss to get in the cab. "Now, let's split back to your crib."
"I have to warn you, my roommate is a bit of a ladies man." Hunter added.
"That doesn't scare me." Ella did become a bit nervous about it, since Hunter was her man and the threat of outsiders made her insecure.
"We'll see. He's got a different punani every night." Hunter was nervous that his roommate Whiz would be banging some random chick right in the living room.
"As if!" Ella was not convinced.
"I'm serious, he's all that and a bag of chips. The dude is a real playa." Hunter replied.

"Whatevs. I'm down with it. Really, I just want a place to crash so we can get to the match tomorrow. I don't care where I'm at." Ella said.

*We finally get to hear one of their many 'great' jokes and it's a doozy. 'In the bag'? You're better than that Ella. Hunter LOVES it though. He laughs loudly! We finally get the 'I love you' moment out of the way and Ella blushes again. She says 'Tsk' which is weird. THEN - after some badly worded kisses – she says (and I honestly can't believe a woman would say this with a straight face) 'let's split back to your crib.' WHO ARE YOU? What have you done with Ella? If his roommate is the ladies man – why does that threaten her? It's got nothing to do with Hunter. Ella's afraid that there will be SO MANY women at their place that the spill over from his roommate's bed will somehow land in Hunter's lap.*

*Did you…oh my… Hunter…did you just use the term 'punani' to describe women in front of your girlfriend? What is happening here? His roomate's name is 'Whiz' and clearly Hunter HAS walked into the house and seen him 'banging' some random in the living room before if he's this concerned about it. It's a common thing. Hunter's a totally different guy now. Is he having a stroke? NO ONE has said the phrase 'He's all that and a bag of chips' in real life have they? The ghostwriter is trying to channel the 90's I guess… 'The dude is a real playa' This writing is WACK, yo.*
*Ella – ever the wordsmith – says 'whatevs' and that she just wants a 'place to crash.' This sleepover is now officially the least romantic thing in the world. It could have been special but now it's like they are just friends sharing a car ride in the morning.*

## Chapter 5

Several more weeks go by, and they celebrate their two-month anniversary. The stigma surrounding Hunter reminded Ella of the match between him and Buster. The way the crowd received Buster into the arena was the same way Hunter was being received. She also started noticing how his behaviors in the ring were starting to match his behaviors outside of the ring. Ella's on stage persona Obsession was rude, and in charge. But off stage she was submissive. It was beginning to clash with her work, and she didn't like the way he commanded her around. Whether or not she didn't like it or if Obsession didn't like it was hard to tell.

*Well they were dating for a month last chapter so... several weeks is four weeks? Four weeks go by to get them to the two-month mark. Is there a stigma around Hunter? Are her friends judging her? It would be a good detail to have. The rest of this paragraph is all over the shop. Both Buster and Hunter are being received the same way by the crowd – so they are being booed? Obsession is a rude character – TOTALLY different from her day to day life – and that's beginning to clash with her work? WHAT work? Ella quit her job! And now Hunter is commanding her around apparently? And now she is referring to herself and Obsession as two different entities. Maybe Ella's got multiple personalities...*

"Babe?" Hunter called from his bedroom.
"What's up?" Ella said, entering the bedroom.
"Can you make me a sandwich?" Hunter asked, politely in a non-joking manner.
"Of course, babe. I'll be right back."
"Babe?" Hunter called from the room again.

"Yea?" Ella shouted from the kitchen.

"I don't want to yell, can you come here?" He loudly said.

Ella, aggravated, returned to the bedroom. "Yes?"

"I was just thinking that it might be better if we ate out instead." Hunter was genuine in his statement.

"Do you not like my sandwiches? What the eff?" Ella has switched to full on Obsession personality.

"Fine, make me a sandwich then. I thought it would be nice if we ate out." Hunter didn't mean to insult her, but to ease the situation figured maybe she should make the sandwich.

"No, let's have it your way. Let's eat out. Where do you want to go? We don't have a lot of money, you know. You haven't been taking all the jobs I've been suggesting." Obsession was truly frustrated, and managing his decisions.

*Are they living together now? Not sure. This is the strangest fight anyone has ever written. Hunter wants a sandwich and then immediately decides they should eat out. He doesn't want to yell so he's making Ella come to him as he lies around in his bedroom. Why don't you make your OWN sandwich Hunter? Instead of feuding over bread. Also she's somehow become his manager? Despite having zero knowledge of the world of professional wrestling she has been trying to book him fights AND he's been turning them down? Hunter is probably contracted to wrestle for the federation he is working for. They pay the bills – although as Ella points out – they don't have alot of money between them. So why on Earth did she think this was a good idea? She QUIT her job for this. This sandwich fight will haunt my nightmares. It's bizarre.*

"For real? Why are you so ghetto right now? I've got enough bones for some fast food." Hunter had been saving money for a while, so he could move out and get a place with Ella.

"No no no, please. The Hunter wants fast food, so let's go catch some shall we?" She started getting her shoes on and preparing to leave. Obsession's personality was one of insult and injury. When she was out for blood, she meant it.

"Woman, chill. I'm okay with the sandwich. I like your grub." Hunter was not quite sure how to handle Ella off stage. He stayed in the bed, hoping to resolve the situation casually.

"You know what? I'm fed up with this crap. Every time I get an idea, you either gank it or you grind it. I just want to have a normal relationship and I joined you to help you wrestle, not to be your house pet. I'm done." Ella grabbed her purse. "I'm done with all of this. With you, and Obession." She slammed the apartment door as she left. Whiz came out of his room naked, with two girls in his bed, scratching his head.

"Dude what the eff man?" Whiz said.

*So much to unpack here! 'Bones' is slang for money. 'Why are you so ghetto' asks Hunter in the MOST ghetto way imaginable. He wants to move out and get a place with Ella – cos it's going sooooo well! Hunter calls her 'woman' in such a disrespectful way. 'Ella it's alright...It's FINE. I'll eat the sandwich. You may make me one now.' And he's having the whole conversation from his bed. Is Ella just inventing words now? You either 'gank it or you grind it.' What does this MEAN? I don't think this is working out either. Ella has realised her mistake and is walking away. Good for her! If a door slams that's enough for Whiz to leave two girls in his room and come out nude to investigate. 'You seem busy Whiz...'*

*'Nah I'm not doing anything important. What's going on with you man?'*

Whiz and Hunter have a strange relationship if this level of nudity is normal. Are the two girls waiting for him? Or is it normal for him to wander away as he has here?

"I'm clueless, dude. The bitch just got mad after I asked her to make a sandwich." Hunter was slightly in shock, and angry. "I don't know what her beef is."
"Jeremy, you need to lighten up dude. That chica is good for you. I heard the whole thing." Hunter got up and went to the living room. "I'm sure the whole building did. She freaked out, dude." Whiz sat on the couch.
"I don't know dude. She was hella pissed. I felt like we were back in the ring and she was doing a bit." Hunter stood, dazed.
"Homey, you need to go get her back. She's probably confused." Whiz grabbed the bong on the table and started packing the pipe.
"That's some junk. She's the mad one!" Hunter didn't move.

Whiz seems like the PERFECT guy to have this conversation with. He'll know what to do! Oh and Hunter? Don't call Ella a bitch. Have some class buddy.
This name-calling doesn't make Hunter any more charming to the reader.
It sounds like Whiz has been eavesdropping doesn't it? 'I heard the whole thing,' he says. I hope the walls aren't thin. Ella has probably heard a lot from Whiz too. In real life Jeremy is my older brother's name so it's interesting that the ghostwriter chose that. It's just a weird coincidence I suppose. How does Whiz know that Ella is good for Hunter? What is he basing that on? Oh no... he's... yep... Whiz SAT ON THE COUCH. He's still naked! Come on man... put on some sweatpants or something! Whiz's advice? Will it be helpful or profound?
'Go get her – she's probably confused.' So it's all her fault. Women! Am I right? Go smoke another bong Whiz. You're the confused one.

"Dude, buy her some ice and tie the knot. You can trust Wizzy. I know a good one when I see it." Whiz finished packing and lit up immediately.

"No way! That's not cool, dude. I don't manage your hook ups." Hunter said. After finishing his toke, Whiz said, "She ain't no hook up, yo. That's a real bad honey you got." He exhaled the smoke, filling the room in a thin haze.

"I'm lost, dude. What went wrong?" Hunter sat down on the couch.

"Take a hit, homie. Let Wizzy explain." Hunter grabbed the bong and took a long, slow hit. "Jeremy, when you first brought Ella back to the apartment, I told you I'd keep my distance. I've kept that promise. Now, you've had your first argument, I'm gonna fix it." Hunter held his breath and sat back after placing the bong back on the coffee table. "She's confused man. Like, the whole scene is just crazy. She loves you, dude. Like, she's not a pigeon. She ain't a shady bitch, neither. You feel me?"

*Get married? Have they been intimate yet? Marriage will solve all of your issues wont it! Whiz is soooooo wise! Trust Wizzy! He described her as a 'real bad honey.' And that seems to be a good thing? I guess in the 90's when we called things 'bad' we really meant they were good. Maybe we've misjudged old Whiz. He's a believer in true love. He's just searching for his 'bad honey' two at a time so he finds her faster. Imagine how awkward it would be if he found her during one of his many threesomes. 'Here Hunter – get stoned. Then my advice will make more sense.' Hunter asked Whiz to keep his distance. Was he afraid Whiz was going to steal Ella? Now Whiz wants to FIX things? She's...not...a...pigeon... what does that even mean? Ella's not just any bird? She ain't 'shady' so she won't cheat on Hunter? Do I feel you? If I could work out what the heck you were talking about maybe I would 'feel' you Whiz. Should I have gotten stoned before reading this? Was my ghostwriter stoned when he WROTE this?*

Hunter exhaled. He thought a moment, letting the situation sink in. Whiz could be right. "Dude, but why would she freak out over a sandwich."

"It's not the sandwich, homie. It's you." Whiz grabbed the bong.

"What about me?" Hunter just sat, looking at the ceiling.

"It's like, your attitude." Whiz lit the bong and took another long drag.

"I do feel like the real Hunter talks to her, instead of me." He sat, reflecting.

"That's what I'm saying, yo. It's your attitude." Whiz exhaled slowly, making a poor attempt to blow smoke rings.

"Maybe I should quit wrestling, then. I love her." Hunter got the bong from Whiz, and took his own hit.

"Dude, that's harsh. But if you think she's the shit, worth dipping on the job, do it. I'm all about that." He paused. "Would be sad to wrestle without you, though." Whiz sat back and started staring at the ceiling.

"Maybe she is worth it." Hunter exhaled and stared at the ceiling.

*The sandwich represents you Hunter. So wise Whiz! So Hunter's solution is to QUIT wrestling? So they have even LESS money and future prospects?*
*'All you need is love' as The Beatles sang. We've also just learned that Whiz is a wrestler too. Maybe we could have learned that before this moment. Why hadn't that come up? It was in my original pitch but it's been executed so badly that I forgot he was supposed to live with another wrestler. They could have met at the arena. Whiz could have wrestled in front of Ella. It's an important detail.*

Ella had left in a hurry, but slamming the apartment door made her feel better. The cab ride back to her own apartment wasn't too bad either. She thought Hunter was being a complete jerk all the time, and dealt with it because she loves him. The old cab driver took note of the young woman's concerned expression and commented.

"Rough night?" The old man said.

"I don't want to talk about it." Ella said.

"Fair enough. I'm a father, you know? I've seen my fair share of boy trouble." The old cabbie was trying to be helpful.

"I don't want to talk about it, alright?" Ella was getting even more frustrated.

"Okay, okay. I'll back off. But I've seen you two together a few times now. If I can help, even just to beat that kid's ass, you let me know, okay?" The old man motioned to the baseball bat in the front passenger seat.

"Thanks, but I'll be alright. I can take care of myself." Ella stared out of the window.

"A strong girl. I know you'll be alright." The old man remained silent, as did Ella.

*They seem to do nothing but take taxi's everywhere. No wonder they don't have much money. And the wise old cab driver is back, which is surprising. He mentions that he's a father – IS he Hunter's father? He seems to loiter outside their apartment as if he's following the saga of their lives. Is he a God-like character that is trying to steer them in the right direction? He keeps a baseball bat in the FRONT seat? Where are we Gotham city? How would you swing a bat at someone in the backseat anyway? You can't. It's not a useful weapon to use inside of a car.*

Whiz and Hunter sat in the living room, smoking for a few hours while Ella went home and slept. Hunter needed to decide whether the title was worth Ella's relationship with him. He considered what they had together, and talked it over with Whiz. The management of the wrestling gig wanted Hunter to be a bad guy, and it was making him be a bad guy even outside of the job. It was even making Ella be a bad girl.

The upcoming match was going to be the title match, where he would be crowned the champion. His opponent would be Buster. The options were simple. He could keep wrestling, and lose the girl he loved, or he could stop wrestling and try to win her back.

"Why can't I just lose the title and be with the girl?" Hunter asked Whiz.

"Because, dude. She would see wrestling as a competition for your attention. She wouldn't be down with it." Whiz waved his hands around in the air as if he were directing a symphony.

"I don't understand females." Hunter was confused and anxious.

"Nobody does, dude. You think I would have so many bitches here if I understood females? I don't even understand myself, homie." Whiz amazed himself. "Yo, that was some deep philosophicalizing dude. I should be a ..." Whiz lost his train of thought and paused a moment. "What was I talking about?"

"I don't know man. I just want Ella back." Hunter was focused on the ceiling, still.

"Oh right on, dude. Where is she?" Whiz was completely lost with the conversation.

Hmmm... does Hunter want the championship belt or does he want Ella? There is no way he can have both! I cannot stress strongly enough that wrestling is FAKE. So neither Hunter nor Ella seems to be able to separate their personas from their real lives. Both are bad / heel characters in the ring and therefore are bad in real life. It's acting! It's performance! Hunter asked her for a sandwich and Ella said 'sure babe.' WHAT IS THIS FIGHT ABOUT? They were fine a minute ago.

Whiz is so stoned he's getting lost in pot holes. The faceless 'management' want Buster to lose to Hunter – making him the champion. But even if Hunter loses the match that's not good enough for Wizzy.

Whiz decrees that Ella would always view wrestling as 'competition' for his attention. It's not new – he was doing it when you met. It's not as if he's suddenly taken on this hobby that now takes up all of his spare time.

And wouldn't you ask him to stop serving drinks in a THONG before you ask him to stop wrestling? Professional wrestling seems like it's his identity! He's Hunter more than he's Jeremy. These characters feel like they are speaking nonsense.

Dropping the Belt is turning into an extremely unrealistic and convoluted story idea. It's hard for me to know if my initial idea was 'off' – leading to this ghostwriter's flawed execution – or whether they have misinterpreted things. Are all of the ingredients I asked for there? Hunter is a topless waiter and he revealed himself to be a professional wrestler. Ella has taken on the role of his valet.

But now they are fighting over sandwiches and things are getting off track.

## Chapter 6

Ella woke up to three messages on her voicemail. She had muted her phone before going to bed, fearing that Hunter would call. For her, any contact with Hunter would disrupt her process of cooling down. Working with him and being his partner outside of work was a treat. The roleplay during the matches was fun, and being a caring girlfriend otherwise was also fun. She really enjoyed the time they spent together.

His muscular body kept her eyes glued to him every minute they were together. The fact that she was with him and other girls were jealous gave Ella an advantage. Most of the other interested girls flocked to try and be near him before and after the matches. For Ella, they were working, so her back-off attitude really worked.

*Find another adjective. Not everything is 'fun' all the time. Ella seems to treat Hunter like a piece of meat. I'm guessing they STILL haven't been intimate? We would have heard otherwise right? 'Babe...lets wait until we have our own place. Then we should totally do it.' What a strange speed this relationship moves at. Ella enjoys getting rid of all of the interested girls. When I made my wrestling documentary The Young and The Wrestlers in 2007 I learned that the term professional wrestlers use for women that loiter around, hoping to sleep with them is 'ring rats.' Gross huh? Just some 'fun' trivia for you dear reader.*

But Hunter was something of an animal as well. Photo opportunities were a time when Ella had to submit if girls wanted pictures with him. That fueled her anger at their presence near him. It was to the point that Ella was quite protective of Hunter. She belonged to him outside of the venue, but he belonged to her in the venue. The dizzying tumble between the two mindsets sometimes crossed over.

Ella wondered if her anger towards him, over a sandwich, was real or not. She listed to the voice messages while she thought about that. All three messages were from Hunter. Each one was more apologetic than the last. The first message was a simple apology. The second was a rationalised argument with an apology. The third message was from his heart. Hunter was confused about his next decision. Ella understood that she still needed to participate in the last match as a valet, despite her anger towards Hunter. She thought maybe she could channel that frustration into her act.

*'You've paid for a photo with Hunter? Alright...not much I can do about that.'*
Ella's coming off as very jealous and possessive here. Obsession seems a fitting name for her now! The balance of power in their relationship is weird too.
She 'belongs' to him outside the ring and he 'belongs' to her inside it? That's an insane way to view a relationship. She thinks the fight was about a sandwich – and nothing more. Ella should talk to Whiz! He'll clear it all up for her! And then he'd gladly take a sandwich as compensation. Oh wow...the way we learn about each message Hunter left! *'...and that third apology that he gave was juuuuusst right.'*
*'Use your imagination but they were very apologetic and heartfelt, okay?'*
Ella's woken up and despite three nice messages she's still angry with him.
She said she was done with Obsession but I guess Ella is contractually obliged to participate? Who knows hey? Some more details would definitely be welcomed.

Confused about what to do, Ella called up her old roommate Amanda. They spoke at length about how she met Hunter and what they've each been up to since the hen party. At the end of the call, Ella received the advice she needed. Amanda told Ella to give the man a choice. If Hunter wins the match, and goes full on bad guy, to leave him. If he loses the match, he must go back to being a good guy and she'll stay. The words only confirmed what Ella had previously thought, but the reassurance from her old roommate was comforting.

*Hey! Amanda's back. So Ella and Amanda haven't spoken since the hen's party over two months ago? Amanda could be married by now! Ella is a very bad friend and now I get why she wasn't going to get an invite to the wedding. So Amanda is giving HER advice and she's taking it? Two options huh? Either let Hunter (as a heel character) win the belt – in which case Ella will leave him – or if he loses and remains a good guy character she will stay with him. So she's letting the result of a 'fixed' wrestling match decide her relationship? It's so weird. If he loses - he's still wrestling. Didn't she want him to quit altogether? As long as he's not the champion it's all okay? The logic here is...stupid. There are many more options.*

A day passed, but Ella didn't return any of Hunter's calls. He left several more messages asking for Ella to call back. She deleted them all. Hunter was busy preparing for his championship match, while Ella was looking through ads in the classified section. She'd hoped she could find a job in a similar field to advertising, but figured she could do any kind of writing job too. The wrestling gigs payed enough to keep her in her apartment, even though she spent a majority of the last month at Hunter's apartment.

*She's been paid SO MUCH from being his valet that she's been able to keep her apartment? Huh? Ella should probably talk to Hunter, am I right? He's trying so hard. Is Ella really worth all this trouble? Looks like it was a bad decision to quit your job then. Good luck finding something Ella. It's a shame all of your 'contacts' from the party haven't heard from you in over two months. You're priorities are wild.*

Hunter showed up to the arena for the match. This was his true test. The whole day he thought about the events that would unfold. Many times he wanted to just quit cold turkey. He thought about just not showing up at all. That wasn't like him, though – and it would only reinforce the bad guy persona. Some fans would probably take it as an insult, the ones who still had hope for the good guy Hunter. He thought about showing up and forfeiting the match, but the result would be the same.

*He thought about just not showing up at all? Both of these characters are so unlikable. They want to quit everything. Can you imagine if he didn't show up? 'Hey Buster have you seen Hunter? No? Oh well...I guess Whiz or Kong will get the title shot instead.' And an even dumber solution? Arrive and forfeit the match. What a competitor! Why do we want good things for Hunter when he's like this?*

Confused and feeling lonely, Hunter stuck to his routines. Being a badass meant showing up whether he wanted to or not. It meant working out when he was sick, or during a holiday. The old good-guy Hunter showed mercy and compassion. He needed to do the same for himself. He granted himself an opportunity for rest, taking it easy when buffing up before the match. When the 30 minute warning arrived, he was fully focused on the match ahead.

*There is a crew member whose only job is to give everyone thirty minute warnings isn't there? Some matches go for less than thirty minutes though...so how on Earth are you timing this? Wrestling isn't scheduled so perfectly. The next match starts when the one in progress ends! These wrestling shows have a kind of 'flow' to them. Things are always happening. Is that the Dictionary definition of a 'badass' by the way? Being a badass means working out on Christmas?*

*'Sorry... I know it's the holidays...but as you know I'm a badass. I'm off to do my workout!'* Why is he *'buffing up'* before a match? I know the writer means that Hunter is working out but the way it's phrased makes him seem like a car again. Do you really believe he is *'fully'* focussed? It sounds like he's thinking about Ella if you ask me. By his own admission he's *'confused and lonely'* too.

The management offered for Buster to throw the match in Hunter's favor, should he agree to fully convert to a bad guy. While Hunter felt almost natural in the persona, even living it, he wasn't fully confident it was the right thing to do. There would always be good guys and bad guys, but the women who loved him for being a bad guy were a different group than the ones who loved him for being a good guy. Ella was there for all of the drama. Ella was a part of the drama. Ella was Obsession, and Hunter was obsessed with Obsession. He hunted it down, captured it, nurtured it, and loved it. He did that with Ella as well.

*The faceless management are back and still negotiating what will happen. It's so badly written by the ghostwriter though. 'I'm just not sure pretending to be bad is a good move for me. Even though it's fake and I'm totally pretending – I'm a good guy deep down.' Some girls like bad guys...other girls like good guys...thank you for the lesson. WHAT AM I READING HERE? There are three sentences in a row that start with the word 'Ella' too...*

*But it gets worse somehow! I would have thought that was impossible. 'A Hunter hunts...and an Obsession obsesses...' This is all awful. Why am I laughing so hard? I shouldn't be enjoying this bad writing so much...but I am!*

"Ladies and gentlemen," the announcer could be heard from backstage. "Please keep your valuables secure. If you love it, don't let go or it will be hunted. Weighing in at 225 pounds, standing at an incredible six-foot one-inches tall, and ready to capture what he's looking for..." the announcer dragged out his name. With an elongated 'the' and a dramatic Hunter where the 'er' is held for 10 seconds, Hunter exited the backstage area and entered the arena. The packed audience held a deafening roar for him, knowing his future potential in the industry. Mixed applause and boos found their way past him as he did his signature creep up and on to the ring.

*Okay...so The Hunter is a kleptomaniac now? No wonder he's a bad guy. The ring announcer is implying that The Hunter will steal your belongings! Is this a common thing he's been doing? Did Ella know about this? The crowd cheers because he has so much potential in the industry. Shouldn't they cheer for Hunter because they like him? Wait...they are booing him too? Oh make up your minds! Now his 'creep' to the ring is a signature move. Yikes.*

Hunter was handed a mic by one of the crew members. "I don't know about you. But I'm obsessed." The crowd cheered. "I want something," he turns to Buster and points, "and you have it." The crowd roared in suspense. Hunter felt in his heart that he was talking about Ella. "The only way I know how to get it," Hunter paused, "is to beat you to your knees and take it."
"I think I should Busta' move then, huh? Show you what I'm really about. You can't hunt me if you can't catch me." Busta kept a stoic serious face on for the crowd. Both he and Hunter knew this was part of the act, but the real wrestling was about to begin.

*This is the first time we've heard Hunter actually speak with a microphone to the crowd. 'You can't hunt me if you can't catch me' is a stupid phrase. Isn't hunting someone the pursuit of them anyway? You CAN hunt someone and not catch them. I'm not impressed with this back and forth really. Neither of these two should be speaking to the crowd. They remind me of the professional wrestler Brock Lesnar. He is physically impressive and looks like an imposing character. Wrestlers like that can carry a franchise. But just like these two, Brock Lesnar struggled with the soap opera elements like speaking convincingly to the crowd. They should have a manager (or valet!) to do the talking for them. That's how they got around the issue with Brock. He let his fists do the talking and had a very successful career.*

The announcers interrupted their standoff. "What's this? Is that Obsession?" said the first announcer.

"That definitely is, and she looks pissed!"

"She's got the angry eyes, Mac. Look at the vengeance on her face!"

Buster saw an opportunity and commented, "Oh, you want your girlfriend to come get the belt for you? Well I ain't no sucka. If you want it, you have to beat me, not her."

Hunter was stunned. "What are you doing here, Obsession?"

A crew member gave her a mic as she made her way to the ring. "I'm here to get you that belt. It's what you wanted right? You're ... Obsessed with it, aren't you?"

*So Ella decides to show up as Obsession. Is that really such a surprise? I guess the ring announcer is named Mac? And I love that she has 'the angry eyes.' There are some layers to what she's doing here I suppose. Ella's appearing to help Hunter win the belt because that's what she assumes he wants. But in doing so she's proving that he loves wrestling more than her. Is that accurate?*

*Can I suggest a drinking game? Drink every time they say their wrestling names 'Hunter' or 'Obsession.' Buster demonstrates that he knows the rules of wrestling. 'You have to beat me – not her.' Yes... that's how it works. You are the champion Buster. You must lose the match in order to lose the belt in this scenario. Sigh...*

The act was both personal, and playing perfectly into the good guy/bad guy plot. Hunter realized her tactic. "I'm obsessed with both of you."
"Don't you want to win, baby?" Ella smirked.
"I'm going to win. I'm the Hunter, and I get what I want." The crowd jeered.
"Well, we all know what you really want, don't we?" Ella looked around at the crowd.
Buster felt left out, so he said, "This Belt!" causing the crowd to spike with laughter.
Ella and Hunter embraced for a kiss, but paused right before their lips touched. She could feel his rapid heartbeat and the tension of a conflicted man. "Then win this match for me, and I'll be your one true Obsession, forever." She broke away from the embrace and shoved Buster out of her way as she exited the ring.

*He wants it all – the belt and the girl. So the crowd is jeering Hunter now? They are booing Buster AND Hunter? Why did they even show up to watch this if they hate it so much? What are they hoping for? A double knock out? When Buster shows the prized championship belt the crowd bursts out laughing. They HATE it. This whole professional wrestling show is a joke to them! Hunter and Ella almost share a kiss – but it's like a foreign act to them – have they only kissed the ONE time? They still haven't been intimate and they don't really know what they are doing with each other. I can't explain the speed of their relationship at all.*

"Looks like somebody's got some Hunting to do!" Buster practically sang his statement, again leading the audience on in laughter.

Hunter threw the microphone off stage and started pacing, waiting for Buster to be ready. The man knew how to take his time, just enough to bring even more tension to the match ahead. Ella stood near the corner of the ring at the ground level, knowing full well that she wouldn't keep her promise to Hunter.

The two wrestlers found themselves grappling immediately after the bell rang. Buster whispered into Hunter's ear, "I will throw the match if that's what you want. But management doesn't want Obsession to be your valet anymore."

*Buster is singing his lines? He doesn't see how this is a joke. Why is Hunter waiting for Buster to be ready? It's supposed to be the championship match! Get the jump on him while he's unprepared and get the advantage. You're a heel now! Ella is planning on helping him win the belt before she leaves him. She is planning on walking away from Hunter and all of this. Management – the faceless entity we have never met – STILL haven't decided how this ends! Wrestling isn't usually made up on the spot like this! Management don't want Obsession as his valet anymore. They will give him the championship as long as she's out. It sounds like Hunter and Ella are both going to get what they want...*

Hunter launched Buster across the ring with a guttural yell not heard by anyone before. He was releasing his true emotions, the pure animalistic rage he held inside. The release of the pent-up fury was invigorating. Every hair on his body stood straight with anger. He lunged at Buster, pinning him to the corner. Hunter whispered back, "We just had a fight, I don't think she's going to stick around anyway." He slapped Buster a few times before the old champ escaped.

The pair danced around the arena for a moment before grappling again. Buster managed to get Hunter into a full nelson, and whispered, "I don't really care, am I throwing the match or not?"

*Hunter's true emotions find their way out in a guttural yell? Why does he have so much rage? Is it because he's sexually frustrated? 'Pent-up fury' might actually be pent-up feelings. Hunter is a white hot ball of rage but as they move into the corner he's rational and disinterested in saving the relationship. 'We had that one fight over a sandwich so...I'm pretty sure it's over with.' Buster is trying to work out what he's doing. Spell it out Hunter! Buster needs to know what to do next...*

Suddenly, and unexpectedly, Buster was blindsided by Obsession with a chair. Her participation was not part of the script that night. Ella had been practicing her showmanship, so she knew how to hit Buster to prevent injury, but maximize the effect. The crowd went wild, cheering uncontrollably. Hunter fell and rolled off to the side. Buster went down, for the show.
Obsession kept hold of the chair, and was now facing Hunter. The pair were in a face off. The deafening sound of the audience became muted white noise. Hunter stared down Obsession. Their eyes locked, as they danced slowly around the ring. They were communicating through their eyes. Obsession's eyes spoke the words "trust me" while Hunter's spoke the words "are you sure?"

*Alright...IF Obsession hit Buster with a chair the match is over. And she did. So it's over! That is a disqualification and Buster should retain his championship belt. This is not a sanctioned hardcore match so weapons are not allowed. Her participation was 'not part of the script' that night? Duh! But ALSO they haven't worked out what the script IS! They are still trying to figure out who will win.*

*But – like I said – the match is over now. It doesn't matter what happens next. Hunter can 'trust' Ella all he likes but he's lost. I don't know why the crowd loves this. They don't know what they want from one moment to the next do they?*

Hunter rushed in first, grabbing at the chair before Obsession could complete her swing with it. He was too powerful, hoisting the chair high, for Obsession. She immediately stumbled backwards into the corner of the ring. He had her pinned in place. Buster was secretly watching from his position on the floor, feigning a concussion. Hunter looked around at the crowd, unable to really hear them, then looked at Obsession. Her wanting eyes determined to get a piece of him suddenly looked away.

The dominating good-guy Hunter threw the chair out of the ring. He let go of Obsession's hands and grabbed her chin, forcing a kiss. They held that kiss in their passionate embrace for what felt like hours. They explored the intricacies of the other's mouth, letting their first real kiss be both public and intimate.

*This is their first REAL kiss? What is happening??? Ella quits her job and wants to move in with a guy she's barely kissed? This is insanity. Does she have a head injury? Did she fall down at the hen's night and this whole story has been a dream? The kiss felt like it went for HOURS to them. What a gross description about 'exploring the intricacies' of eachothers mouths. Yuck. So much tongue!*

Buster jumped up and grabbed Hunter. He backed away with his hostage, taunting Obsession with Hunter's demise. She exited the ring. Buster whispered again if he should throw the match. Hunter tapped Buster's arm with two quick pulses of his thumb, their personal code for 'no'. Buster chopped Hunter's shoulder, and released him. Hunter fell limp to the ring floor, feigning a concussion of his own.

Obsession screamed with rage. Her man was down. But she didn't want Buster to take the victory. She rushed the stage while Buster was pumping up the crowd, and pinned Hunter. The referee was unaware if this was part of the script or not, so he dives in and starts counting. "1... 2..."

Obsession whispered, "Don't move, just take it. Shhh"

"4... 5...6..." The referee continued.

Hunter whispered, "What are you doing?"

The referee was almost done counting, "8... 9..."

"Saving your dumb ass." Obsession said.

"10..." The referee waved around that the match was complete, raising Obsession's arm as the victor. Buster, confused but playing along, came over and raised Obsession's other arm. Hunter remained on the ground, pretending to be knocked out.

*Buster recovered quickly didn't he? Unless their kiss actually went for hours! And he's STILL asking Hunter if he should throw the match. They have a personal code for 'no' and it's TWO taps with the thumb? Buster is saying full sentences and Hunter can't whisper 'no' back to him under his breath? Hunter 'feigns' a concussion on the floor after he's hit...in the shoulder. Wow. What. An. Actor. Obsession doesn't want Buster to win? Too bad she already handed him the victory by hitting him with a chair and disqualifying Hunter. Ella's going to...pin Hunter? So she doesn't want Buster to win but does want Hunter to LOSE? Also – and this is a big one – when the referee counts a pinfall in professional wrestling he only counts to THREE. Not all the way to ten. This is not a boxing match where they are counting a knockout. These are just the basic rules of wrestling and I'm not sure that the ghostwriter knows them. And at the end Hunter's still acting concussed from the same shoulder injury. That's commitment...*

## Chapter 7

"I still don't understand what happened." Buster said.

"I saw a fourth option," Obsession said. "I could get more involved and be evil."

"Whatever it was, management is happy." Kong chimed in. "You did good. Er, evil?" They all laughed.

"So, Obsession, welcome to the team. I don't suppose you're looking for anyone at the moment, are you?" Buster asked.

"Well, no, not yet. I guess this makes me a free agent." Ella laughed. "But outside of work, I'm dating Jeremy."

"Wait, how do you know my real name?" Hunter asked.

"No, not you. Another Jeremy." Obsession said.

"Hold on, you've been dating another guy while we're together?"

"What can I say, I'm addicted to men." Obsession smirked.

"Unbelievable. You're a real piece of work, you know that?" Hunter raged.

"Oh, please. I've known your name was Jeremy for a while." Ella said. "Your buddy Whiz has a big mouth."

*Wasn't Obsession already an evil character? This wasn't a change. It seemed more like Ella was betraying Hunter than siding with Buster. They seem to be a team based on the arm-raising in victory. Were there THREE options presented earlier? I remember TWO. So Ella's invented a FOURTH option when there were two outcomes. Okay... Kong reappears to tell us that management is happy with this? What about this makes them happy? Hunter was pinned by his female valet, who was not an active participant in the match, and who actually caused his disqualification. So Buster is still the champion and the crowd didn't get what they wanted, right? What about this scenario is a happy ending?*

*Ella is a free agent - meaning she could valet for anyone now. Hunter is perplexed that she knows his real name and that she's been paying any attention to him at all. He's also a moron who doesn't understand sarcasm. Hunter's infuriated when she jokes about being addicted to men. He's in a confused rage!*

"So you're not dating someone else?" Hunter asked, throwing his hands up in confusion.

"Of course, not sweetie. You're the only Jeremy for me." She leaned over and put her head on his chest. She could hear his rapid heartbeat thumping away. That joke definitely scared him. The group drank their beers and told jokes as the night calmed down.

All other wrestlers seemed to be on board with Ella participating the way that she did, congratulating her on her first victory. The tradition with a first victory was to dump a bucket of cold water on the winner, but the guys weren't sure how they could do that. Instead, they hazed Obsession by randomly dunking cubes of ice down the back of her shirt for the whole night. They were like a big family, just as Hunter claimed, and now Ella was a part of them.

*Hunter...sit down sweetie. Okay... let's clear up this totally confusing sequence of events. Your name is actually Jeremy. Ella likes Jeremy. That's you! Ella likes you. The end. All of the other wrestlers are HAPPY about Ella's level of involvement? It's like NOBODY knew how that match should have ended so they were just glad that somebody did something. They are congratulating her on a victory that is not technically hers! Buster won the match. Obsession wasn't competing for the belt. 'Instead of dumping cold water on her let's taunt her all night with ice cubes.' Yeah... that's better.*

Jeremy and Ella found themselves back at his apartment, laid in bed, cuddling. Hunter had a moment of realisation.

"I would drop my belt for you." He said.

"You don't have a belt to drop, babe." Ella smirked.

"Yea, but if I ever did get one, I would leave it all behind…" He paused. "For you."

"Awe, you're so sweet. I love you." Ella leaned in and they kissed. "You might have to fight me for the belt, you know."

"Wouldn't that be a great show? Me beating Obsession, for a title win, in front of all our fans?" Hunter daydreamed.

"It might be, but I have to get the belt first." Ella thought deeply. They sat in silence thinking about the glory ahead.

*What a pair of idiots! Hunter's willing to lose his championship belt to Obsession, provided he ever gets one. In professional wrestling men don't traditionally fight women for championships – or at all. If they lose it makes them seem weak in wrestling circles. They have a division of women that fight eachother to solve this issue. Men and women fighting is considered a novelty. Sometimes they'll solve this by having a 'mixed' tag team match, which means a man & woman team up against another man & woman. Do Hunter and Ella HAVE fans? I remember a bunch of people booing them. Neither of them is a champion. They also seem unable to consummate this relationship!*

"You know, if we keep this up, we could both have a belt." Jeremy said.

"How so? There's only one, but I'm down." Ella's confidence was uplifting.

"We could team up again to beat Buster. And you could be, I dunno, a spy or something." Jeremy explained.

"If you take on Buster, and we have a rematch in a few weeks, you could set up a trap for him and I'll step in. We just have to pin him together."

"Oh, you are evil, aren't you? But are you as evil as me?" Ella forced Jeremy on his back, pinning him to the bed.

*How can you BOTH have a belt if there is only ONE belt? Hunter has taken too many hits to the head I think. A spy? WHAT ARE YOU TALKING ABOUT? Why would Hunter – the savage beast character – ever be a SPY? How would his being 'a spy' help in ANY way toward either of you getting a belt? Would you pin Buster together? Did management just decide to let these two do whatever they like? They are making the decisions for the whole company now? This ends very poorly too. Ella pins him to the bed. The ghostwriter behind this work wanted an open-ended piece so that I would order more words from him. That much is clear. He did specify a cliffhanger but this just seems like he reached his word limit and stopped.*

Right… so was that money well spent? Keep in mind it was only $25 for the words you have just read through. Did I get less than ten thousand words? Sure. But they were so bad that I couldn't help but enjoy them for their stupidity. I gave the writer a good review and thanked him even though he'd offered unlimited revisions until I was happy. In a way I *was* happy with his work. It was hilarious to me. I just had no idea what the heck I should do with it. It was too bizarre to rework and made me feel as if the entire idea was a bit silly. I put it away and forgot about it.

I brought it out a few times as a joke and was pleased and validated when other people laughed at the absurdity of it too.

## PART TWO

I finished my time travel novel *The Glove* and felt a surge of pride. Writing the whole thing had taken me almost two years but I'd done it. It had been about ten months since I'd paid the first ghostwriter for *Dropping the Belt*. It had been a while and I wanted to read those words again. I found the work of the first ghostwriter in a drawer and laughed just as hard. It was so amusing to me that my idea had been interpreted the way it had. It was certainly different! I thought about publishing it as an E-book in its current form and letting others enjoy it but it felt *unfinished* somehow. It needed more.

To my delight I realised that this was only the *first* part of the story of Hunter and Ella. I felt I owed it to these fictional characters to see their story through. I decided that I would repeat the experiment twice more and that *Dropping the Belt* would be written as a kind of ghostwriter trilogy. Part one was now complete. Maybe Hunter and Obsession *could* both have a belt someday!

All I really knew was that I had discovered something that amused me and that I wanted to see it through to the end. I decided to use the initial part as the jumping off point for the second part. The first ghostwriter was no longer on the website and there were no clues as to why he'd disappeared. That left me no choice. I'd need a new ghostwriter to continue the story. I commissioned another ten thousand words with a fresh voice! I decided on a female ghostwriter living in a different part of America. Her profile claimed that she had many literary credentials and promised she could churn out the required work in only a week. I messaged her and updated her on the story but left out the fact that she would be writing the second part in my professional wrestling trilogy.

**ME:**

Hi there. I wanted to see if you were interested in writing ten thousand words of the following story. The story is about Hunter (Male, muscular Blonde – whose REAL name is Jeremy) and his girlfriend Ella (Brunette and athletic) who are both working as professional wrestlers. He wrestles as the character 'The Hunter' (in cheetah leggings) and she wrestles as 'Obsession.' Back when they first started dating he introduced her to his passion (professional wrestling - the fake kind) and she loved it. Ella quit her writing job to do it. NOW in present day they are popular in the wrestling federation they work for and are regularly recognised in the street. People talk about them online and management loves them! Hunter becomes the champion at the start of the story. While they are wrestling at a big event later on 'The Hunter' hurts himself in the ring and is forced to lose the match and his belt. Ella accompanies him to the hospital afterwards and they learn he will not be able to wrestle anymore. She continues to wrestle as Obsession while he comes to terms with his loss (Hunter was very passionate about wrestling) and she finds other male wrestlers are into her – attracted to her and hitting on her – now that Hunter isn't around as much. She has to choose between wrestling and Hunter in the end.

I also described the side characters that the first ghostwriter had introduced while encouraging the new writer to use her imagination and expand on the story.

**GHOSTWRITER #2:**

I like the idea, and think I could work with it. You would own all commercial rights.

**ME:**

Do you have a time frame? Any orders in the queue? Any questions?

## GHOSTWRITER #2:

I don't have any others I'm working on. I think I could do it in a week.

This ghostwriter asked me *zero* follow up questions. She didn't care to flesh out the characters and unfortunately the price point had increased to $45 for ten thousand words. Would a higher cost mean better attention to detail? I hoped that – like the *Godfather* film series – the second one would be the best.
I had no idea what to expect all over again.

One week later as promised my ten thousand words was delivered. As I never gave the story an actual title the second ghostwriter called her work "ESTACY OF THE HEART." The spelling mistake has been left in for authenticity.
Also (possibly to increase the word count) the delivery had an elaborate contents page at the start that looked like this:

    CHAPTER ONE.........................................HUNTER'S POINT OF VIEW

    CHAPTER TWO.........................................ELLA'S POINT OF VIEW

    CHAPTER THREE....................................HUNTER'S POINT OF VIEW

    CHAPTER FOUR.......................................ELLA'S POINT OF VIEW

    CHAPTER FIVE........................................ELLA'S POINT OF VIEW

    CHAPTER SIX..........................................HUNTER'S POINT OF VIEW

    CHAPTER SEVEN....................................ELLA'S POINT OF VIEW

And so on and so on all the way through to Chapter Ten.

What would be next for Hunter and Ella on their quest for professional wrestling glory? I dove into the ten chapters eagerly. Again – to best illustrate to you what I received from this second ghostwriter – I have not corrected any spelling or grammar from the original delivery. I have once again added my own thoughts in *italics* as I did for the first ghostwriter's work.

Fair warning to you dear reader… even though I didn't *ask* for erotica here… I didn't *not* ask for it. The second ghostwriter has taken certain liberties and I wanted to give you a heads up so that you would be ready for it. The story is taking a much more adult turn here. Not that penis paraphernalia wasn't adult!

# CHAPTER ONE

## HUNTER POINT OF VIEW

It was raining hard today and I was driving more like speeding so I could go on the match on time. I saw a traffic light and stopped the car when a woman outside gasped.

I cursed because I literally made her wet. I got out and she groaned. "What the hell watch were you're going." She said and I sighed.

"Okay chill I'm just rushing somewhere I didn't see you." I said and she sighed. "Whatever." She said and walked off. I rolled my eyes and got in the car again and drove off.

I made it at the place were I was having my match and I got in the dressing room and got ready. "What took you so freaking long?" Ian said and I rolled my eyes. "Chill will ya? I just got stuck in traffic." I said and he nodded.

*Did Hunter JUST learn the word 'chill'? He's gotta stop saying that. It's not really clear what has happened in the opening lines but I'm assuming (because of the rain) that Hunter drove through a puddle and it splashed up which literally made that girl – who was walking nearby - wet. Hunter wasn't just driving along while she became spontaneously aroused, right? There is a lot of sighing here too. People seem a little... off. I'm assuming Ian is a kind of manager at 'the place' where he's having his match. They seem quite hostile with eachother don't they?*

"Ladies and gentlemen today we have an important match. Two of our best fighters are going to fight against each other. On one side we have Hitman that has lost three matches only." I heard the presenter and I chuckled.

"Make them four." I said and Zayn chuckled.

"On the other side we have Thunder that has broke record and haven't lost a single fight." He said and I heard everyone cheer and I walked out.

After the match I won of course but I was hurt badly at my back and kidney. "Fuck he was good motherfucking fighter." I said and Ian nodded. "But you are better so get up and let's go at the hospital." He said and I groaned.

*The name 'Hitman' makes me think of former champion Bret 'The Hitman' Hart. He's a Canadian wrestler who was involved in a famous feud with Vince McMahon, the Chairman of the WWE. He wound up spitting in his face – but that's another story. I'm just saying it's not a very original wrestling name. Who is Zayn? Is Zayn the wrestler known as Hitman? So Hitman has only lost three fights? Out of how many? Without context this doesn't really mean anything! 'Make them four' is the first major sign that this second ghostwriter might be from a foreign country too. Unfortunately the ghostwriter has renamed Hunter as 'Thunder.' I don't know why as I was pretty clear on the character names when I explained the concept. Maybe this too was lost in translation. She skipped over all the wrestling and honestly I don't mind that much. It's supposed to be more about the relationship between Hunter/Thunder and Ella anyway. Hunter's undefeated too? How does he know he hurt his back AND kidney? That's very specific! Hunter is just very aware of his own body I suppose. Even his internal organs.*

"Do we have to? I don't wanna look like a pussy." I said and Ozan rolled his eyes. "You are such an idiot." He said and I punched him and he winced and rubbed his arm.

"Let's go." Ian said and we went at the hospital. A nurse walked us at a room and she said to wait for the doctor.

"Hello." I looked up to see the woman I accidentally made wet and she looked at me. "Oh look at that." She said and Ian with Zayn walked out of the room. "Lemme see what you have." She said and came closer.

Now that I'm looking at her closer and better she was pretty hot. After she gave me some ice and a cream she told me I could leave. "Uhm I'm sorry about earlier." I said and she chuckled.

"It's fine and I'm actually sorry for being that steep before I was just mad with something." She said and I nodded. "Well thanks again." I said and she nodded. I left the hospital and after that everyone wanted to celebrate at a club my win.

*'If you have internal injuries and then go to the hospital you'll look like a pussy.' Who is Ozan? Is that meant to be Ian? It's hard not to be critical of the obvious errors in spelling and grammar. It's the big reunion of Hunter/Thunder and the woman he made wet. I like that the two other guys left the room as soon as she walked in. She was kind of 'steep' before wasn't she? That's the right word isn't it? Steep. And as a nurse she gave him amazing treatment for his back and kidneys didn't she? Ice and a cream? 'And you know what else is good for kidneys? Drinking! Off to the club to celebrate my big win!'*

We were at the usual table I took a sip of my drink while looking at girls dancing. "Omg it's Hunter." I heard a girl say and I turned and chuckled. "Or else Thunder." I said and winked at her.

I was having fun when girls knew my name and would like to be all up on me. "Dude those girls over there are eye-fucking you." Zayn said and I chuckled. "But no sex for you these days." Ian said and I raised an eyebrow.

"And why is that mum?" I asked and he rolled his eyes. "Because I say so. You have to be careful with girls. You never know what story they will sell at the media and then in seconds your whole career is over." He said and I shook my head.

*So this ghostwriter is actually intentionally calling him Thunder? Why? He's being recognised as Hunter too, which makes it even more confusing! I like how she says 'Omg' too – not 'Oh My God' but 'Omg.' That probably says more about the girl in the club really. Ian thinks Hunter is too famous and powerful to be sleeping around. If he sleeps with the wrong lady they will alert the media and his career as a professional wrestler will be over. Is Ian looking out for his best interests?*

Ian always acted like my father and it get's annoying at times. He can't tell me I can't have sex I have needs too. "Well damnn isn't that the doctor from the hospital today?" Oliver asked and I turned and spotted the same woman from today.

The third time I'm seeing her today. "She is hot dude." John said and I nodded. "Is she all alone?" Zayn asked and I chuckled. "Not for a long time." I said and stood up walking towards her.

I arrived at the bar and she looked at me and chuckled. "How many more times are we going to meet for today?" She said and I chuckled and shrugged. "I don't know. Maybe we can just give it an end here tonight." I said and she raised an eyebrow and took a sip of her drink.

*So Ian acts like his father but Hunter called him 'Mum'? More random guys are featured here. Who is Oliver? Who is John? What are the odds of seeing the same woman in the morning in the rain while driving, then again later at the hospital and now at a nightclub? Is it a small town? She's worked all day and is having a big night out? I don't buy it. Their flirting is damaged by the poor use of the English language here. They are going to 'give it an end here tonight.' What is that supposed to mean? It sounds very final and very ominous to me.*

"Our acquaintance wasn't that good so let's make this right. I'm Hunter...Hunter." I said and she nodded. "I'm Ella...Ella Grace." She said and I shook her hand and smiled.

"Lemme cherish you a drink." I said and she held her glass pointing at me. "I already have one." She said and I went closer. "Tonight we might need more than one." I said and licked my lips.

She gave me a teasing smile and nodded. "If you say so Mr Jeremy." She said and I was honestly getting turned on. Her red lips were looking so kissable that I just wanted to smash my lips on hers.

*Ugh... this is hard to read. My apologies again dear reader. Even though I asked this ghostwriter to continue the story of Hunter and Ella they have given them a brand new meet-cute. They were supposed to be dating already. The writer has also given them last names. She's Ella Grace and he's Hunter Hunter. Huh? That can't be right can it? 'Cherish you a drink m'lady?' It's astoundingly incorrect. She's calling him Jeremy too? I mentioned that it was his real name but if they are meeting here for the first time then how does Ella know it? Mr Jeremy? Like famous porn star Ron Jeremy? What an awful description of wanting to kiss her. He wants to 'smash' his lips on hers. That's very violent. This is not a promising start to the second part of the trilogy.*

I got us two more drinks and we drunk. "Wanna continue the party at my house?" I wishpered in her ear. "Okay then. Lead the way." She said and I smirked and grabbed her hand.

We got in my car and I drove us at my house. "That's a nice house." She said and I nodded. "Why are you living so far from town." She asked and I opened the door and she walked in.

"Because I like having my privacy." I said and she nodded. We walked in the living room and she looked around. "Want some wine?" I asked and she turned and nodded. "Red wine please." She said and I nodded.

"Coming." I said and took two glasses and poured red wine. I then walked in the living room and handed her a glass and I took a seat next to her. "I think I'm already drunk." She said close to me. She was so close that I could feel her breath.

*Ella's pretty trusting! She knows so little about this guy and he buys her one drink and she's going home with him. It's a 'nice' house. With no description of it at all! If Hunter lives so far from town did they just spend like an hour in the car? Wouldn't that be weird for Ella? If she met this guy and he drove for an hour or so? I'm speculating about the time but wouldn't she become fearful at some point? Lots of nodding their heads. Even if she was drunk at the club they've just been driving for such a long time that I would guess Ella would have sobered up by now.*

I chuckled and she took a sip of her drink again. "I've never seen you before around where have you been?" I asked and she giggled.

"I have recently moved here." She said and sighed. "For what work?" I asked and she bite her lip and nodded. "Sure you can call it that." She said and I nodded. Of course I wasn't going to sleep with her yet.

She was just teasing me all the way tonight but she didn't look like the girl she would like to wake up next to me the next day.

*So... to defy Ian and prove you can do what you want you WON'T be sleeping with her? What's the point of bringing her home then? And Hunter asks Ella about work. Her response of 'sure you can call it that' makes it seem like she might NOT be a nurse or doctor. It implies that it isn't the work she does. I mean... not a strong start from ghostwriter number 2. Hopefully it improves.*

## CHAPTER TWO

### ELLA POINT OF VIEW

I was at work and after a while I finished and grabbed my stuff and walked out. I didn't have friends here because I just moved so I didn't have plans. I sighed and started walking towards my house. The weather was again bad and it started pouring and I groaned.

"Need a ride?" I turned to see Hunter and I tried to keep myself from smiling. "What are you doing here?" I asked and raised my eyebrow and he shrugged. "I was passing by and I saw you. It started pouring so get in I will drive you home." He said and I got in his car.

"Thanks." I said and he smiled and started driving. "So when did you move?" He asked. "It's been a month or so." I said and he nodded. "That's cool." He said and I looked out of the window. After a while he pulled over and I turned at him and smiled. "Thank you for the ride." I said. "Wanna come in?" I asked and he chuckled and nodded. "Sure I have nothing to do anyways." He said and we got out of the car but it was raining hard so Hunter put his jacket up and pulled me close to me and we run at the door step.

*An entire shift in that first sentence! Nothing notable happened at work then? Ella doesn't give him any directions or indication as to where she lives. Hunter seems to know though – like a stalker! She doesn't have plans and he doesn't have plans. It seems very convenient that they ran into each other if you ask me.*

We made it there and I giggled and he chuckled too. I opened the door and we walked in. "Your house is warm." He said and I smiled. "I will go grab towels you can go relax in the living room." I said and he nodded.

I walked upstairs and grabbed two towels and walked back downstairs in the living room. I handed Hunter a towel and he took it and started drying himself. I did the same then I sat next to him.

"Want something to drink or eat?" I asked and he shrugged. "I don't wanna be a bother." He said and I stood up and chuckled. "You are no bother." I said and he stood up as well. "Can I take a shower?" He asked and I raised an eyebrow and he just looked at me.

*'Your house is warm' makes me think Ella left the heater on. She is very hospitable when she fetches them towels. Then she offers Hunter something to 'drink or eat' and it sounds weird to me when it's that way around. I've always said 'eat or drink.' Is it just me? He doesn't want to be a bother...so he'll just use the shower? What kind of rain did he get caught in? It wasn't like he was working out. He said he had nothing to do – so why is he so sweaty already? Is this a pick-up technique?*

"Okay yea sure let me show you where the bathroom is." I said and started walking and he followed. I walked in my room and he walked in as well. "You can take a shower in my bathroom the other one is not working." I said and he nodded. "Okay thank you." He said. I grabbed a towel and handed him. He walked in the bathroom and closed the door.

I walked downstairs and started cooking. After I made the food I walked upstairs and knocked on the bathroom door. He wouldn't answer so I opened the door to see him with a towel wrapped around his waist.

I almost slapped myself. He looked up at me and raised an eyebrow. I didn't want to admit it but I was horny. He walked closer and I felt my legs weak. He pushed me against the door and started kissing my neck. I bite my lip and wrapped my arms around his neck. He then kissed me and I kissed him back while playing with his hair.

*Ella brings him up to her bedroom? I see where this is going. I laughed when it said she 'handed him.' That sounded too sexual. Ha! She went downstairs and made a meal. How long was his shower? And then Hunter's not responsive afterwards. He went straight for the neck too. Like some kind of vampire.*

He then bite my lip making me give him entrance. He put his tongue in and I moaned. He took off my shirt and bite his lip. He also took my jeans off letting me with my bra and panties. "Jump." He whispered at me making me shiver and I jumped in his arms wrapping my legs around his waist.

We walked in the bedroom and he laid me down on bed. He hovered over me and started rubbing my legs while kissing me. I moaned and he played with my panties and put his hand in my panties and started rubbing me. I groaned in pleasure and he ripped my panties off. I flipped us over and took my bra off and Hunter bite his lip and came closer and started sucking my breast.

I groaned and he flipped us over so he was on top and I bite my lip. He placed a finger in and I held on him tightly. "Fuck." He said and I groaned again. "Hunter." I moaned and he placed a finger again making me moan louder.

*He says 'jump' and she jumps. It's like...she's a dog or something. Maybe Ella's a submissive and likes being told what to do. This writing got very sexual suddenly. It's erotica even though we never discussed the genre of this. I guess I should have in retrospect! There is a bunch of moaning and groaning here. Also this feels very unearned. This feels like lust. They haven't bothered to get to know eachother.*

He then looked at me and smirked licking his fingers. I looked at his towel and took it off. "I want you." I said and he kissed me then pushed himself in making groan. "H-harder damn it." I said and he did what I said. "Hunter I'm gonna-

"Fuck me too." He said and after a while we cum and he laid next to me breathing heavily. I then got on top of him and started kissing his neck. He started moaning and I smirked. I started rubbing his dick and he moaned. "Fuck." He said and I started playing around with his dick.

After a while we just laid in bed looking at the ceiling. "That was hot." Hunter said and I giggled. "That's what first came to your mind?" I said looking at him and he chuckled. "I just didn't know what else to say." He said and I chuckled and looked up at him resting my head on my hand.

*Yep...a bunch of sex. This is what ghostwriters assume you want I suppose.*

"For a fighter you are not that aggressive when it comes to sex." I said and he looked at me and smirked. "Maybe some other day we can try that." He said. "I'm hungry we should go eat the pasta." I said and grabbed Hunter's shirt putting it on. He grabbed his underwear and pants and we walked downstairs.

"Wanna eat in the kitchen or living room while watching a movie?" I asked him and he wrapped his arm around my waist kissing my neck. "Living room." He said and I smiled and pulled away. "Okay now big boss." I said and handed him his plate. "Want something to drink?" I asked. "A beer." He said and I nodded.

We then walked in the living room and sat on couch. I looked over at Hunter that was watching TV while eating and I smiled. It looked like we were husband a wife. Crazy huh?

*I don't know… Hunter seems kind of aggressive to me. He initiated it when Ella walked in by pushing her into the door. I guess their dinner is pasta…and it's surely cold after all of their sex. She's claiming him by putting on his clothes. Ella wants him to remain shirtless I guess. It's her house and it's not like he has any other clothing options there. I suppose they are going to watch a movie then. They really didn't have any plans, did they? Why does she call him 'big boss' anyway? Is this the end of a video game or something? Is Hunter the final boss on the last level? Doesn't he have enough nicknames at this point? And then she imagines them as husband and wife? That's pretty fast. Maybe Ella's the weird one…*

## CHAPTER THREE

### HUNTER POINT OF VIEW

I walked in the gym and groaned. "Look who finally decided to show up." Ian said and I rolled my eyes. "Don't fuck with me I have a headache that can kill people around me." I said and he rolled his eyes.

"Where have you been?" He asked. "What are you my dad?" I said and raised an eyebrow. "Hunter quit the jokes what the hell did you do? Where were you???" He said again.

"I was just out." I said and grabbed my gloves. "No shit Sherlock." He said and I started hitting the punching bag. "Just leave me alone so I can get ready for tonight." I said imagining that Ian was the punching bag.

*Hunter has a headache that is SO bad it might kill other people? I actually think that's great. Why does Ian care where he was? I'm guessing he's late to training. But he asks 'what did you do' as if Hunter is covered in blood in this scene.*

"Tomorrow you have a photoshoot for Health and sport magazine." He said and I shrugged. "Great." I said. "Just be careful what you do we don't want the pictures that will be taken to be with hickeys and shit like that." He said and I smirked. "They can edit that part." I said and he rolled his eyes again. "Just shut up and work." He said.

"Ian you shut the fuck up you know I don't like people treating me like shit so fuck off." I said. "Where is Zayn anyways?" I asked. Better him than Ian. At least Zayn shares weird ass stories of him and girls and makes my training more like a play time.

*Ian has a real vendetta against Hunter having a girlfriend. Maybe he was hurt in the past? Hunter explodes at him here claiming he doesn't 'like people treating him like shit' but who DOES? And IS Ian actually treating him like shit? We also learn that Zayn has 'weird ass stories' and likes to share them. Great.*

"He is running late." Ian said and then we heard Zayn. "Did someone mention my name?" He said and I chuckled. "Okay Ian Zayn is here thanks bye now." I said and he walked off.

"What's up with grumpy pants again?" Zayn asked and I chuckled. "Ian just being Ian." I said and he nodded. "Where were you British dick?" I asked and he chuckled. "I was fucking a crazy bitch. I thought she was normal hit and miss but no she had to be crazy and follow me and start saying she likes me and all those shits." He said and I chuckled. I remembered my night with Ella. That was even more hotter and better than any other night. She was a hot and smart woman.

*Zayn is here now so... BYE IAN! Zayn is British I guess? And the girl he describes sounds crazy doesn't she? She expressed that she liked him! Crazy! Ella is described here as 'hot' AND 'smart' which is every guys dream, right?*

"That's not cool." I said and he nodded. "Now just keep training Bieber we have to win tonight." He said and I chuckled. "I can win with my eyes closed." I said. "Just be careful not to take a punch or anything or we will have to run at the hospital again." He said.

But that way I met Ella. I mean I saw her again because I had already met her the day earlier. "That was a bonus for the night." I said and he raised an eyebrow. "You are thinking about the hot doctor aren't you?" He asked and I nodded. "She was hot." I said and then kept training.

*And now we're calling him 'Bieber' for no reason. Another nickname? Wrestling is fixed. So if you're meant to win – then you will. And a single punch could send them to the hospital? I'm starting to think this second ghostwriter doesn't understand wrestling either. Ella is described as 'hot' twice more. We don't even know her hair colour – let alone ANY of her physical characteristics! Use your imagination dear reader. Don't rely on the words on the page, huh?*

After a while I was at the place we were playing tonight and I was getting ready. "Yo you know what I need?" I asked and Ian looked at me. "What 1296 bitches to suck your dick while you're beating a guy?" He said and I looked at him. "That would be dope." I said and he rolled his eyes.

"But no I need someone like a physiotherapist. You know just so she can chill me and get me ready for the fight or after the fight so she can just massage me. I have to keep my body and muscles good." I said and he made a thinking face.

*Wow... okay... But why 1296 'bitches' specifically? I mean... with that quantity of 'bitches' they will have an extremely difficult time getting access to your penis. Unless the implication is that he has some kind of supernatural penis that would somehow accommodate the mouths of almost 1300 women. And then – if that wasn't difficult enough – they have to perform said fellatio while Hunter is 'beating a guy.' I hope this refers to defeating a wrestler in the ring and not jerking one off but one never knows with this insanity! 'That would be dope' is his reply. I like that Zayn made 'a thinking face' too. How very ridiculous.*

"That's not a really bad idea." He said and I smirked. "I have just found one already." I said and he looked at me. "Good call him or her and we will talk and then we will see." He said and I grabbed my phone and walked out of the room and called Ella.

"Hello?" I heard her voice and smiled. "Hey there are you free?" I said. "I'm just leaving from work what is it?" She asked.

"I'll send you an adress and come as soon as you can we will talk there." I said and ended the call. I texted her the adress and waited for her outside of the club. After a few minutes she walked there and looked at me weirdly.

*'That's NOT a really bad idea' implies that he thought it WOULD be a really bad idea and that he's surprised that it's not! Isn't Hunter great? He is texting Ella an address and then telling her to go there. Will he wait and see if she's free and able to? No! He's hung up on her and assumes she'll meet him there. Perfect. It sounds like she 'walked there' in only a few minutes so I guess it's no big deal after all!*

"Why are we meeting here?" She asked and I smirked. "I have a suggestion for you." I said and she looked at me waiting for me to continiue. "Listen I'm a professional fighter and I need a doctor or physiotherapist to keep me healthy." I said and she raised an eyebrow. "And?" She said and I frowned. "And don't you want the job? It has good money I'm telling you. Ian pays good." I said and she looked like she was thinking about it.

"Okay but I'm not leaving my job. I will do them both can I?" She asked and I nodded. "Great come on. Ian wants to talk to you." I said and she followed me.

*It's funny that in the first story Ella quit her job to do professional wrestling with Hunter but here she won't quit her job to be his physiotherapist. I like that it 'pays good' too. Based on what? Nobody else appears to have a physiotherapist so it's not something Hunter would know. He's making that up to get Ella to do it.*

After Ian and Ella talked he seemed to like her so he gave her the job. "Are you staying to see the match now?" I asked Ella and she nodded. "I have no other choice Bieber. I'm gonna go get a drink. I'll be in the crowd. Good luck." He said and was about to walk off but I grabbed her hand and pushed her against the wall.

"You can't just go with a good luck." I said licking my lips and she bite her lip. I smashed my lips on hers and she run her hands through my hair while I placed my hand on her hip and my other hand on her cheek. We pulled away when I heard my name being called and Ella smirked. "Maybe you're lucky enough tonight to win Thunder." She said and walked off. I smirked and walked out.

*She gets the job based on a... conversation? Alright... also Ian didn't know anything about this before now. Zayn was the only one there when they decided he needed a physiotherapist. And Ella is calling him 'Bieber' now too? That was Zayn's nickname for him wasn't it? Also she calls him Thunder! What is happening? Why is everyone in this story smirking and nodding so much?*


After the match I was really fucking tired. This guy almost killed me. He is one of the best out there too but not better than me of course. "Ella help." I said and she walked over at me. I was sitting on couch and she came and started massaging me.

"That guy almost kicked your ass." She whispered in my ear because Ian and the other guys from the team were here. "No one can do that." I said and she run her hands up and down my back making me turn on.

"Stop doing that." I whispered. "That's my job Hunter remember?" She said and I closed my eyes just enjoying it. I would love to fuck her tonight but I was fucked up so I couldn't really move.


*Of course he's not better at wrestling than you. You're the best Hunter! Even though we never see you wrestle and you seem hurt and tired all the time. You're undefeated! In fake wrestling. Hunter's so near death that all he can muster is 'Ella help.' So he's backstage at this moment and Ian and the other guys are nearby. Presumably he doesn't want to seem weak in front of them. That was his concern before. And although he would love to 'fuck her tonight' he's too tired. What a catch huh ladies? He can barely move.*

# CHAPTER FOUR

## ELLA'S POINT OF VIEW

I was in Hunter's bed and I stood up getting dressed. "What's all those scars on your body?" He asked out of nowhere and I frowned and put my jeans on. "It's nothing." I said trying to get away with from the question. I couldn't talk about it. Every time I think about it I lock myself in the bedroom.

"I have to go." I said putting my shirt on and shoes and Hunter raised an eyebrow. "Did I say something wrong?" He said and I shook my head.

"No I just have to go that's all." I said and he stood up and walked close to me. "You can't just leave like that." He said and I looked at him and sighed. "Hunter I'm not in mood to stay here." I said and he licked his lips then kissed me.

*Ella's covered in scars and he's only just noticing them now. Captain observant! Every time she thinks about it she locks herself in the bedroom? What? And I don't like how often he's licking his lips. It's kind of gross...*

I kissed him back then pulled away. "I'll see you later." I said and walked off. I sighed and walked at my house. I walked in and locked the door. I walked in the bathroom and took off my shirt looking at some of the bruises.

Hunter had noticed them of course. I just tried to cover them and then got dressed and walked at work. "Hey Bels." I smiled at Victoria and walked in my office. I took a seat and checked a few files. I heard a knock and looked up. "Come in." I said and the door opened and a Lisa a nurse that worked here walked in.

*Ella walks everywhere doesn't she? Hunter has a car and doesn't drop her off. What a good relationship they have. And don't forget – he lives really far out of town! Ella is probably walking for hours to get to work. No wonder she has to leave in a hurry! She says hi to 'Bels' before smiling at 'Victoria' and then seeing 'Lisa.' What is the point of any of this? Who are these people to us anyway?*

"Mrs Ella we have an Emergency. You have to come." She said and I stood up and followed her rushing. "Ian?" I asked confused. "My fiance is in there do something." He said and I nodded and rushed in.

After a while I walked out and Ian rushed at me. "How is she?" He asked. "She is fine. It looks like she went through a miscarriage and they haven't clean her up good." I said and he sighed and nodded. "Thanks." He said.

"You can go see her now and she can leave the hospital in a couple hours." I said and started walking off when I bumped on someone. "Hunter?" I said and he sighed. "How is Kayla?" He asked.

"She is fine." I said and he nodded. "Damn you have no idea how fucking hot you look with that uniform on." He said and bite his lip. "Hunter what the hell?" I wishpered and he pulled me closer placing his hand on my ass. I pushed his hand away and he looked at me.

*Alright... lots to unpack here again. Ian is there and he's engaged to Kayla. She's just had a miscarriage. She's fine though – even though she's a mess – and can leave in a couple of hours. Why did they need to grab Ella for this? Hunter goes from compassionate friend to horny teenager in ten seconds! He doesn't care that she's at work or what that goop is on her scrubs. Hunter's a bit much here.*

"I'm at work you dickhead." I said and he chuckled. "So what? We can go in your office." He said winking at me and I rolled my eyes playfully. "You freak while people here need me you want us to fuck." I said and he shrugged.

"I need you more." He said and I rolled my eyes again. "Hunter just go see Kayla and Ian." I said. "I have work maybe tomorrow." I said and walked off. Hunter was a good man even if he just gets too horny... like all the time. I sighed and walked in my office. When I was done with everything I walked out of the hospital. I walked home and walked in closing the door.

"Welcome home Ella." I jumped scared when the lights turned on and I turned to see him... Caleb.

*Hunter needs Ella more? More than dying people? His sexual needs are greater than those of the sick and injured? The emergency here is in his pants. And she rightfully tries to steer him towards his obligation to Ian and Kayla but then confuses us all by not knowing whether she actually has work tomorrow. Ella walked home again. What is wrong with the public transport system in this city? We are given an introduction to Caleb here. Let's find out who the hell he is...*

"W-What are you doing here?" I asked getting nervous and he chuckled walking closer. "I told you I will find you whenever the fuck you go." He said and I shook my head. "Get the fuck out of here or else I will call the police." I said and he laughed.

"You can't do that Ella. You just can't." He said and came close to me. "You are trying to run away from me but you will never get that. Only when you die honey." He said and tried to kiss me but I pushed him away.

"You can't get out of here Ella." He said and I run upstairs.

*So Caleb's some kind of crazy stalker huh? How did he not 'find her' sooner when Ella's out in the open walking all day long? Also finding her 'whenever' she goes implies she is a time traveller. It should be 'wherever' she goes. She can't call the police? Because she just can't? Solid reasoning from Caleb. Does he want to kiss her or kill her? His motives are all over the place.*

I sighed looking at Ella's contact. I hit call and I waited for her to answer but she didn't. I groaned and just decided to go over at her house.

I drove at her house and pulled over. I knocked on the door but there was no answer till I heard screams. "Fuck." I broke the door and walked in.

"ELLA?" I walked upstairs to see a guy in her room trying to get her out of the bathroom. "Oh great." He said when he saw me. "ELLA WHO'S THIS?" I yelled and heard her sob.

*To confuse things even more we now have Hunter's point of view in a chapter that is meant to be for Ella. He 'drove at her house' makes me visualise some kind of game of chicken that he loses at the last minute by pulling over. These two are definitely going to fight aren't they? Hunter will win as he's a wrestler. Right?*

Whoever he was he was not any good near her. "Get the fuck out of here." I said and he rolled his eyes. "You have no right to tell me what to do you dick." He said and I punched him. "Get the hell out of here and stay away or else I will fucking kill you. You have no idea who the hell I am." I said and he split some blood.

"Okay you know what I'll go for now... BUT I'LL BE ELLA YOU KNOW I WILL." He said and smirked walking off.

I knocked on Ella's bathroom door. "Ella open the door." I said and I sighed. "Come on he is gone just open the door it's just me." I said and the door opened. She looked at me then hugged me. I had so many questions. I needed answers but right now it wasn't the time for that. I wrapped my arms around her and just hugged her back. It's the first time I'm seeing her like that and somehow it made me feel bad.

*YOU have so many questions? Caleb yells 'I'll be Ella' before he leaves. Does he want to BE Ella? What does that mean? And they just let him leave? Hunter punched him once and they let him walk out the door – despite his ongoing threats! Also Hunter broke the door on his way in...so this house is no longer secure. It's the first time you're seeing Ella like this and SOMEHOW it makes you feel bad? She's the victim of an assault! You're damn right you should feel bad Hunter.*

# CHAPTER FIVE

## ELLA'S POINT OF VIEW

After I calmed down I stood up and grabbed a suitcase. I grabbed my clothes and started throwing them in. "What are you doing?" Hunter said walking in my room. "I'm leaving. I have to get out of here as soon as I can or else he will kill me if he finds me again here." I said panicking.

"Woahh woahh woahh. Calm down there." Hunter said and stopped me. I looked at him and he sighed. "Listen Ella I don't know what's going and it's fine whenever you feel like you want to tell me you can tell me. But if you runaway he will probably find you again. Just stay come over at my house. I will protect you. Like damn it he can't even find you there." He said and I sighed and looked down.

*If you thought he would actually kill you why didn't you call the police? Why didn't you ask Hunter to hold him? Or knock him out? Hunter seemed the more capable fighter. Now is the time for Ella to tell Hunter the truth about what is going on. 'Caleb will be able to find you anywhere – except for at MY house!' It's so far out of town that Hunter might be right. Nobody can find Hunter's place. Plus Ella walks everywhere. She's a sitting duck for most of the day otherwise.*

He was right. If I left now he would find me again. "I don't know Hunter if something happens to you I will never forgive myself." I said and he chuckled.

"Nothing will happen to me chill. I can protect myself from a pussy. Now take some stuff and we are going to at my place." He said and I sighed and nodded.

I took some of my clothes and some books and stuff and walked downstairs. "You ready?" Hunter asked and I nodded.

"Great let's go." He said and grabbed my suitcase and placed it in the back. I got in his car and he did too and started driving. "Thank you." I said and he glanced at me and smiled then watched back at the road.

*Ella doesn't want anything to happen to Hunter. Maybe she does love him? That has not been made clear. This pattern of using the word 'pussy' is extremely unpleasant. Ella is letting Hunter push her around here. It seems like such lazy writing for her to grab 'some clothes and books and stuff' here. Like, what books? Why are you grabbing books? What stuff? Something personal and irreplaceable? Ella just nods at everything. It's an annoying feature of this story.*

"It's nothing. Just trying to keep the best doctor in the town. People need you doc." He said and I chuckled and shook my head. "Chill there Thunder." I said and he smirked. "You calling me Thunder makes me so fucking horny." He said and I bite my lip and smiled looking down.

After a while we arrived at Hunter's house and we walked in. "So I have guest rooms but just so you feel more safe you can sleep with me." He said and winked at me. "Let's go." He said and I followed him upstairs. We walked in his room and he chuckled.

"So we can both stay in my bedroom." He said and I nodded. I wasn't complaining. I was kind of scared still.

"I wonder how many girls have you had over in this bed." I said and he chuckled looking at me.

"One." He said and I raised an eyebrow. "Yeah right." I said and he nodded. "Look I know I've fucked a lot of girls but I've never took them in my bedroom." He said and I rolled my eyes playfully.

*How Hunter's attitude has changed! Earlier he and his needs were more important but now she's an important doctor! I thought she was a nurse? Why does he LIKE being called Thunder? None of this has been explained at all. 'Scared still' is supposed to be 'scared stiff' I guess. But Ella is not so frightened that she can't wonder about how many ladies have been in his bed. He tries to be sweet by simultaneously bragging about conquests and making her feel special. Hunter comes off as a player I think. I mean where is he taking all these girls that he is bedding? Must be going back to their places because he lives so far out of town!*

It would get me kind of jealous thinking some other girl touching Hunter. He was like a masterpiece. His hard chest his lips, his hair. And mostly his eyes that made you travel then his fingers. He had those kind of perfect long piano fingers.

"You're eye fucking me again." He said and I smiled and took off my shirt. "Can I have one of your shirts? They are way comfortable." I said and he chuckled. He took of his shirt and passed it at me.

*Hunter has 'travelling eyes' and is described as a masterpiece. He also has 'long piano fingers' which I guess would be a good feature. But he is a wrestler. So I think his hands would be callused and rough from training and physical activity.*

"There you go princess." He said and I put on his shirt then took off my jeans. "So when is your next fight?" I asked and he groaned and laid in bed. "It's in two days. But my back is killing me." He said and I smirked and got on top of his back and started massaging him.

"Ohh dammnn." He moaned and I smiled. "You're hands are magical doctor." He added and I giggled. "You are such a weirdo." I said and he moaned. "I'm a hot ass weirdo." He said and I shook my head smiling.

*A 'hot ass weirdo'... I have no words for this nonsense. It's all over the place.*

"Hunter how did you decide to be a fighter?" I asked out of nowhere just wanting to know him more. I moved away and he sat up pulling me on his lap. "In High school I met some friends that weren't really great friends. I was hanging out with them and they would have those fights called Street Fights. Once I just tried it and I was good at it. The guys pushed me to fight every day after that. I liked it. I felt like I had the other person in my hands.

After that I never stopped. It's like a drug you know. It's what I like to do." He said and I nodded. He was hiding something but I wasn't going to make him tell me. I was hiding a lot too. Maybe that's why we are just perfect for each other.

*So Hunter used to do street fighting and that somehow led him to wrestling? Who is he Zangief from Street Fighter? This doesn't really make sense. They have definitely misinterpreted the kind of fighting this story was supposed to be about.*

"Why did you become a doctor?" He asked and I smiled and looked down at him playing with his fingers. "When I got sick really serious I spend a lot of time in a hospital. I looked at all those kids there and the doctors that were trying their best to save them. It made me want to help everyone. That's when I decided I was going to be a doctor one day and I would try my best to save everyone. I don't want money from this I just want little kids happy and everyone else to be okay." I said and he smiled.

"Now you are such a good person ." He said and I chuckled. "I try." I said and he nodded. "Do you believe in fate?" I asked and he raised an eyebrow. "I don't know. I'm not the kind of guy to just believe in like love at first sight or stuff like that." He said and I nodded.

"I think I believe in fate." I said looking at him. "I think people really do meet for a reason." I said and nodded. "Maybe you're right." He said.

Maybe me and Hunter we didn't meet accidentally. Maybe it was meant for us to meet.

*What were you sick with Ella? What a vague backstory. She's not in it for the money. Also I feel like she's trying to force Hunter to fall in love with her. I still find their dynamic so odd.*

# CHAPTER SIX

## HUNTER'S POINT OF VIEW

I was at the gym doing push ups when Zayn walked in. "Well look at Thunder." He said and I chuckled. "Don't play with me right now Ian told me I have to just freaking work out extra today because I have the fight later at the night." I said and he nodded eating some cookies.

"Where did you get those?" I asked and he chuckled. "Oh yeah Ella was passing by and she forgot you had a fight and she just gave me the cookies she had made." He said and I groaned and rolled my eyes.

"I hate when she doesn't give me what I want." I said and he laughed. "I like her. You should keep her." He said and I rolled my eyes.

"By the way is she coming at the fight?" He asked and I looked at him. "I don't know." I said and he hummed.

*Both ghostwriters have portrayed these wrestlers as pumping iron the day of their fights. Wouldn't this be a risky tactic? What if they hurt themselves and can't fight that night? Or strain themselves and lose? This was an issue in the last story too. Ella doesn't 'give you' what you want Hunter? Did you want cookies? What on Earth is she withholding from you? She's already moved in with you. She's sleeping with you. What's your problem Hunter? What expectations do you have of her? Maybe if Ella HAD quit her nursing job to be your physiotherapist?*

"What's going on with Ella?" He asked and I looked at him. "What do you mean?" I asked and he chuckled. "Uhm well you took her in your house and looks like you're after her like a pussy." He said and I stood up.

"Shut the fuck up I'm not after her like a pussy." I said and grabbed the gloves. "Aha whatever makes you sleep at night. But hey it's fine to like a girl." He said and I rolled my eyes. "I don't like girls so." I said.

After the work out I drove over at the hospital where Ella is working and I walked in. I walked in her office and she looked at me. "Hunter what are you doing here?" She asked and I chuckled and locked the door and walked towards her.

*More of the 'P' word. And a weird confession from Hunter about not liking girls! Maybe that dialogue is meant to be from Zayn? Is he gay? If Zayn is gay then his 'weird ass stories' from earlier take on a new meaning. Why is Hunter driving over to the hospital now? He has a fight that he's supposed to be preparing for.*

"I was working out for hours and I have a fight after a while so we better do something." I said putting her close to my body kissing her neck. She groaned and pulled away. "Hunter I'm at work." She said and I groaned and looked at her.

"Fuck that they're other doctors here Ella." I said and took my shirt off. "Omg you are a sex addict." She said and I started kissing her neck again taking off her shirt. "Fuck it then." She said grabbing my neck kissing me.

*Oh he's going to be tired and he'll have nobody but himself to blame when he loses his match. His attitude to her job changes yet again. 'Someone else can save lives today! I'm more important Ella!' Hunter might be a sex addict actually.*

I groaned and placed her on her desk. I took off her jeans and started rubbing her leg. She placed her hands on my basketball shorts and I groaned.

I pulled away and took of her bra biting my lip. "If someone knocks or w-

I interrupted her with a kiss and she moaned. I pulled away and smirked. "That's why you should at least be a little quiet babe." I said and she and cupped her one breast making her moan. She took my basketball shorts off and I groaned. I took off her underwear and she groaned. "Fuck it just come already." She said and I took off my underwear pushing myself in.

"FUCK." She moaned and I groaned. "As much as I love you moaning louder and louder we shouldn't get caught now baby." I said and she groaned. I pushed myself deeper and she kept quiet but she kept moaning. "I'm gonna-

She didn't make it to finish her sentence and we both cum. I groaned and looked up at her and kissed her. She wrapped her arms around my neck and kissed me. "Damn that was hot." I said and grabbed my clothes. We started getting dressed and Ella chuckled. "Well let's just say that was the first time I did that on a desk." She said and I started laughing.

*SO. MUCH. MOANING. AND. GROANING. Ugh... Not a fan of this at all.*

She giggled and I shook my head. "We are so weird." I said and she nodded. "Yeah I agree." She said and put on her shirt. "So are you coming at my fight tonight?" I asked putting my shoes on.

"I don't know I mean it gets me kind of nervous." She said and I looked at her. "Why?" I asked and she shrugged. "I don't know I just don't like seeing others in pain." She said and I chuckled. "Okay you're way too soft right now." I said and she rolled her eyes playfully. "Well then we'll see I might come." She said and I nodded. "Okay great I gotta go now. Ian is calling me again. I have to go at the gym." I said and she smiled.

*Now they are BOTH weird. For wanting to have sex? And now Ella doesn't want to come to his fight because of her backstory? She never had an issue with it before. And he's going BACK to the gym? He's been working out for hours so far!*

"Okay see you later." She said and I kissed her again and she smiled through the kiss. "See ya." I said winking at her. I then opened the door to see a nurse close by and Ella cleared her throat. "Just take the medicines I gave you." She said and I smirked. "Of course thanks doc." I said and left. I went back at the gym where Ian was waiting for me. "Great where were you?" He asked.

"I had a break so." I said and he rolled his eyes. "Yeah a break to rest not go play games." He said and I chuckled. "I'm gonna go I still have to work out."

*Ian can't control him. And Hunter is coming off as a real jerk here.*

## CHAPTER SEVEN

### ELLA'S POINT OF VIEW

I arrived home late tonight because I did a double shift. I walked in the living room to see Hunter sleeping on the couch. I smiled and walked closer and shook him softly. "Hunter?" I said and he moaned making me bite my lip.

"Hunter wake up." I said and he opened his eyes and rubbed them. "What time is it?" He asked. "It's about 11." I said and he groaned.

"Ian killed me at the gym today." He said. "I see. Let me make you dinner real quick." I said and he grabbed my hand and stood up placing me close to his body. "I sure am tired but you can relax me." He said kissing my neck and I pulled away. "Nah pretty boy." I said and he groaned.

*No mention of the match so I guess we've jumped ahead again? Ian is really thrashing him at the gym. Hunter hasn't made dinner yet? It's 11pm! Ella hasn't eaten dinner yet? It's 11pm! He's trying to get laid? Ella just did a DOUBLE shift!*

"I'll go change real quick and make dinner." I said and run upstairs. I placed my bag on the couch and grabbed one of Hunter's shirts. I took off my clothes and put on his shirt and walked downstairs in the kitchen. I made some Da Orazio Pizza and Porchetta. "HUNTER ARE YOU COMING IN THE KITCHEN OR WANNA EAT IN THE LIVING ROOM?" I yelled. "LIVING ROOM."

He yelled back and I grabbed the plates and walked in the living room handing him a plate.

"There you go." I said and he smiled. I sat next to him and we started eating. "Damn man how lucky did I get?" He said and chuckled. "A doctor a fucking amazing woman in bed and a great cook." He said making me roll my eyes playfully.

*Does Ella own any shirts or does she exclusively wear Hunter's clothes? Did she heat up leftovers? Or are we meant to believe that Ella made a pizza from scratch? I mean that's fifteen minutes in the oven. Why have they included the brand of 'Da Orazio' here? Apparently it's a pizza shop at Bondi Beach. How oddly specific...*

"This is heaven." He added. "Okay now let's not overreact." I said. "So how is work going?" He asked and I shrugged. "Good I guess." I said and he nodded. After he was done he placed the plate on the table and looked at me. "Listen Ella I didn't wanna ask you from the beginning but you were worried and scared but I can't it's eating me inside." He said and I placed my plate on the table and looked at him.

"What do you wanna ask?" I asked and he sighed. "What happened that day who was that guy?" He asked and I sighed and looked down. "Hunter look I-

"Ella I'm not stupid. It looked like he was your ex or something." He said and I nodded. "He was my ex and the worst mistake in my life." I said and let out a sarcastic chuckle. "I know you're curious it's okay cause I'm basically living in your house." I said and he shook his head.

"I don't wanna pressure you but I'm worried." He said and I looked at him and smiled.

*Let's not overreact? He thinks its heaven. Take a compliment Ella! Or was that about how good the pizza was? How has Hunter waited this long to ask about Caleb? Why is she letting out a 'sarcastic' chuckle? Does she NOT think Caleb was the worst mistake of her life? You are 'basically' living in his house – because you ARE living in his house. He broke your door remember? Why is he worried now? What's changed? Hunter's been nothing but horny since the Caleb incident.*

"Listen I don't think I'm ready just yet." I said and he nodded. "Okay I will be here whenever you're ready to talk." He said and I hugged him. "Thank you." I said and he wrapped his arms around me and hugged me then after a while I pulled away.

"We are staying in and acting as if we're old." I said and he chuckled. "Yeah it's all Ian's fault because he is killing me lately. It's like he is doing it on purpose." He said and I chuckled and stood up grabbing the plates.

I walked in the kitchen and did the dishes real quick when I felt Hunter's hand around my waist and kiss lips on my neck.

"Oh Jay." I said and he smirked. "You in my shirts walking around like nothing is happening drives me fucking crazy." He said and I bite my lip. "We can't do this today." I said and he frowned.

*And she's NOT going to tell him? How is everyone okay with this? They went to a nightclub once. It seems like the regular routine IS staying home. Also, why would Ian want to wear Hunter down this way? I presume Hunter is a drawcard for Ian and therefore makes him money through ticket sales. Maybe we should make a list of all the things that drive Hunter into a 'mad' state. Or would it be quicker to make a list of things that DON'T arouse him? And why is she calling him 'Jay' now? Make up your mind Ella.*

"Hmm who says that?" He said and kept kissing my neck. "I thought you were tired." I said turning at him wrapping my arms around his neck. He smirked picking me up placing me on the counter. "I told you when I see you I don't care how tired my fucking body is cause you make it better." He said and kissed me rubbing my leg. I moaned and kissed him back then pulled away.

"No but literally Hunter we can't do this tonight." I said and jumped off the counter smirking. "This is so unfair." I heard him say and I chuckled. "I'm going to bed." I said and walked upstairs. I got in Hunter's bedroom and laid in bed grabbing my book from the nightstand. Hunter walked in after a while and groaned.

*This is at least the third time Hunter has rubbed her leg resulting in a moan or a groan. What's going on with the sensitivity of her legs? They 'literally' can't do it. Is Ella wearing a chastity belt? Why can't they 'literally' do it? Also doesn't Hunter act like a baby when Ella turns him down? It's not very attractive Hunter. I'd be sick of all the groaning in this household.*

I chuckled and he took off his shirt and walked in the bathroom. "WHERE TO?" I asked. "JERKING OFF OR YOU WANNA HELP ME?" He asked and I laughed. "IN YOUR DREAMS." I yelled and he moaned.

I shook my head and went back to my book. I thought at the time that I couldn't be horrified anymore, or wounded. I suppose that's a common conceit, that you've already been so damaged that damage itself, in its totality, makes you safe.

*Hang on... what? What am I reading? Where is this prose coming from? 'So damaged that damage itself...' that feels almost... eloquent. This is as close to Shakespeare as it's been so far! And to think...that decent writing followed an exchange about jerking off in a bathroom. (Additional Note: Since publishing 'Dropping the Belt' in 2019 I have learned that this quote has been directly stolen word for word from 'We Need to Talk about Kevin' by Lionel Shriver.)*


"Ella?" I snapped out of it and jumped a little scared. "Hey calm down it's just me." Hunter said smiling and I smiled too. "I just was really into the book." I said and he nodded.

"Ya know it's pretty late you should just rest." He said and I nodded. I placed the book on the nightstand and turned the light off. I laid and made myself comfortable when Hunter did too placing me closer. He placed his hand around me and kissed my bare shoulder.

"Good night." He said and I smiled. "Good night Jay." I said and closed my eyes falling asleep.

Hunter tells Ella when it's bedtime. That's pretty controlling isn't it? I guess when you're eating at 11:15 at night, washing dishes, reading and arguing it's 'pretty late' before you know it. This is a BAD relationship. They are both very unlikable characters and there is a severe lack of wrestling in this story so far.

I'm not enjoying the vulgar language that keeps creeping into the work. I don't love the gross and full on sex scenes that she's written either. To be honest I'm not convinced that this ghostwriter is female at all. I think I've been duped once again by an avatar on a misleading profile. I'm not really surprised.

It's just bumming me out that while the first ghostwriter's work felt unintentionally amusing this work is just bad. I wish it was more light-hearted and entertaining but it's just poorly constructed.

## CHAPTER EIGHT

### HUNTERS'S POINT OF VIEW

"Caleb no." I was sleeping when I heard Ella's voice. I opened my eyes when I saw her sweating. "Ella?" I said turning a light on and shaking her softly. "Ella wake up." I said and she sat up breathing heavily.

"Are you okay?" I said and she sighed. "I'm fine it was just a nightmare." She said and I pulled her in my arms. "Okay calm down." I said and her breathing came back to normal after a few.

"Ella are you feeling better?" I asked and heard her sniffle. "Hunter I have to leave." She said and I looked down at her. "What do you mean?" I asked and she pulled away and looked down. "Caleb will find me I can't stay here Hunter." She said and stood up.

*Ella went from 'it's okay' to 'I have to leave' in no time at all. Again, what has changed exactly? She's been safe for a week or two (I'm guessing) at his place. It's not as if an event has occurred to change her mind. Ella seems safest with Hunter.*

"Ella we talked about this. I'm not letting you leave." I said and she sighed. "Caleb is going,

"What is happening with him? Why is he after you?" I said getting out of the bed.

"Ella God damn it just tell me cause if I get him in my hands I will fucking kill him." I said and she looked up at me.

She sighed and sat on bed. "Listen Caleb is my ex and he is not the best guy out there. I decided to break up with him one day and he just went crazy. He told me if he doesn't get me in bed one more time he will just kill me. He is crazy." She said and I looked at her. "The fuck he is mentally crazy." I said and she sighed. "Hunter I should go." She said. "Don't say that again. You're not going. That dickhead can't find you here trust me." I said kneeling down and she sighed and nodded.

*Hunter not LETTING her leave sounds threatening doesn't it? Having no information at all about who Caleb is, our hero has decided that (because Ella had a nightmare) he will kill him if he can get his hands on him. Oh he's 'not the best guy' Ella? Are you sure? He just wants to SLEEP with her once more? And Caleb wants to 'be Ella' by the way. That's his motivation? Oh boy...*

"Great." I said and kissed her forehead. Maybe our relationship wasn't normal. We just used each other for our needs. But I didn't wanna lose her as a friend. She was really caring and different. "Come on let's go to sleep." I said and she sighed.

"Hunter?" I looked at her and she smiled. "Thank you...I mean you're comforting me." She said and I smiled. "Yeah I don't really know how to comfort a girl but I'm trying." I said and she smiled. "I think you're doing great." She said and I smiled. "Thanks."

*Hang on WHAT now? You are admitting this is just about sex? And 'using eachother for our needs' sounds bad. Also Hunter doesn't know how to comfort a girl? The same way you comfort a boy. With compassion and empathy. Girls are treated as if they are 'less than' by this ghostwriter – even though she's female apparently! Like I said: I don't buy it.*

The next morning I woke up to see Ella's side empty. I walked downstairs to see her setting the table. "Good morning." I said and she looked up and smiled. "Good morning." She said. "When did you get up so early?" I asked and took a seat.

"Uhm I uhh." She looked down and I nodded. "You didn't sleep at all did you?" I asked and she sighed. "I'm sorry I just couldn't sleep but I'm better I promise." She said and I nodded. "I made you breakfast." She said and I looked at what she was wearing. She was still in my shirt and I looked at her.

"Aren't you going at work today?" I asked. "No I don't have work today." She said and I smirked. "Oh really?" I said and grabbed her by the waist pulling her on my lap. "You know how about we skip breakfast and just take a hot shower together." I said and she chuckled. "No way we are not skipping breakfast." She said and I pouted.

*Ella is wearing his shirt yet again. He went from concerned about her lack of sleep to super horny. These are real mood swings from Hunter. What's wrong with him? And she is pretty adamant about them not missing out on this breakfast. Maybe she's been up all night making it. And he's pouting...*

"After breakfast we can do something that you want." She said winking at me and I smirked. "Great." I said and we started eating. After that she did the dishes and I groaned.

"Ella come on." I said and she giggled. "Hunter calm down are you really that horny?" She asked and I walked at her and started kissing her neck. "You have no idea." I said.

She turned at me and smirked. "I thought you had to go to the gym today?" She said and bite her lip. "Huh?" I said and looked at her. She giggled and I raised an eyebrow. "Fuck the gym we can work out here." I said and she kissed me. I groaned and kissed her back. She then pulled away. "Yeah but I have plans for today." She said and I frowned. "Wait what? You made me horny as fuck just walking with that shirt around and then you tell me no thanks I'm not buying?" I said.

*There is far too much smirking in this paragraph. Ella is fixated on doing the dishes right after each and every meal. He's into sex and she wants a clean place. Maybe there is a sitcom in this? I think she has some idea of how horny you are Hunter. Sex is pretty much all you want to talk about and do. What plans does Ella have? She stayed up all night. She should be going to sleep! Ella will have to travel into the city for hours and by then she'll be too tired to do...whatever she's planning on doing. Hunter is behaving like an arsehole here. He's claiming that it's her fault that he's so horny. She's wearing his shirt – and that makes him horny. He alleges that Ella is making him 'horny as fuck' and then not having sex with him. This environment is feeling unsafe. Also this story is less and less and less about professional wrestling.*

"I'm sorry Hunter." She said and I groaned. "So now I have to just go at the gym?" I said and she laughed. "Wait with who you have plans?" I asked and she looked at me. "Kayla." She said and I looked at her. "Kayla?" I said and she nodded walking upstairs. I followed her and she started taking her clothes off. "Ella how about we just stay in today huh?" I said walking closer.

And she rolled her eyes playfully and grabbed some clothes. "Hunter I am not a sex machine." She said chuckling. "Hmm." I said and nodded. "I got it we are not having fun today." I said and grabbed some clothes.

I heard my phone ringing and I answered. "What?" I said.

*Poor Kayla. She's been through something traumatic and she just wants to hang with her friend. Hunter is the least sympathetic man in the world. He's preventing Ella from seeing Kayla. He makes more effort trying to have sex with Ella than anything else in his life. Ella has to tell him that she's not a 'sex machine' to get rid of him. And isn't he nice when he answers the phone? Why would we like this character? I feel like Hunter needs so much redeeming here.*

## CHAPTER NINE

### ELLA'S POINT OF VIEW

I couldn't do this anymore. Me and Hunter weren't a couple and I was starting to catch feelings for him. He didn't look like the guy to catch feelings for someone though.

"I'M HOME." I heard his voice and I sighed. He walked in and raised an eyebrow. "What's up?" He said and took off his sweaty shirt. "Nothing much I'm just kind of bored." I said and he nodded.

"Yeah I don't think so." He said and I looked at him confused. "What?" I said and he sighed. "Listen Ella maybe I don't know you for like years but I can tell when you're lying." He said and I sighed. "I-I can't do this anymore with you." I said and he looked at me. "What do you mean?" He asked and I sighed. "This that is going on between us has to stop." I said.

*HOW? How is she catching feelings for Hunter? What has he done to make her love him? He's being a major jerk if you ask me. Love is a strange feeling. He says he thinks Ella's lying and that she's NOT bored! Hunter is telling her how to FEEL now. I love the line 'This that is going on between us has to stop' because it sounds clever. It's sort of poetic. I can imagine it in a daytime soap opera or something. Maybe I like so little of this story that I have to cling on to the small moments of possible brilliance like specks of gold in a river of sludge.*

"But we-

"We are acting like teenagers." I said and he shook his head. "Ella I thought-

"Hunter I can't be your little fuck buddy. I'm sorry. I can leave if you want." I said and he shook his head. "No that's cool. I mean I don't wanna lose you as a friend." He said and I nodded but inside my heart crushed.

As friends...

"Great." I said and he nodded. "I'm going out are you coming?" He asked and I shrugged. "I don't know maybe some other time." I said and he nodded. He walked upstairs and I sighed. After a while he walked downstairs all dressed and grabbed his car keys. "I might come late so don't wait up for me." He said and left. Maybe I was the only one hurting. I mean Hunter could have any woman after all.

*How much time has passed? Another month? Ella's in love with him and Hunter's fine with them going back to being friends. I'm not sure they were ever actually friends to begin with. Hunter's going out now? I hope he took a shower first! Hunter was described as very sweaty a moment ago. So Ella's going to keep living there? I mean... she doesn't want to find herself in a Caleb situation but this environment isn't good for her either. Something has to give.*

I watched TV then I walked upstairs and just read a book till I heard Hunter's car. I opened the door of the bedroom a little when he walked upstairs with his arm around a girl. To say I felt stupid was an understatement.

"Let me show you what's fun babe." She said and Hunter chuckled till he looked up to see me. I smiled sadly and the girl looked at me. "Uhm who's that?" She asked and I looked at Hunter waiting for his answer.

"No one Special." He said and I slammed the door shut. I sat down and cried. I knew he didn't felt something for me. With the first chance he got he went and brought a girl in here where I was staying.

*How many bedrooms are there in the house? Where was Hunter taking this new girl? And doesn't she sound soooo smart? The way the word 'Special' is capitalised makes it seem like the girl is named Special. And she seems it.*

The next day I just packed everything and walked out of the room and walked downstairs to see him and the new girl in the kitchen. "Hey there I'm Catherine." She said and faked a smile.

"Ella?" Hunter said looking at my bags. "Where are you going?" He asked. "I'm leaving. I don't wanna be a bother to you guys." I said and faked a smile. "What are you talking about?" Hunter said and I sighed.

"I'm going at a hotel don't worry. Hope you two have a good time." I said and left the house. I drove at a hotel. I just looked out of the window. He could wait till I left the house to bring someone else.

Okay I get it I'm not the girl of every guys dream but I was a human too and I have feelings too. Why would he do that in front of my eyes. I heard them screaming all night and fucking. I heard my phone and I sniffled and just answered.

*Ella sure walks a bunch... Why is this girl staying there? Because Hunter lives SO far out of the city. Everyone has to stay over. Also – does Ella still have her job as a nurse? Wait... Ella drove away? In what car? Why has she been walking everywhere and receiving rides from Hunter if she has a vehicle available to her? Another game of chicken with the hotel she 'drove at.' She WAS a human? What is Ella now? And she WAS the girl of his dreams! He was saying how lucky he was earlier. She was listening to them all night? 'Screaming and fucking' huh? Great.*

"Mum?" I said. "Honey what's wrong how are you?" She asked worried and I sobbed.

"I'm not fine mum." "Did Caleb hurt you-

"No mum it wasn't him." I said and sniffled. "Then what's wrong honey?" She asked. "Mum why do I always fall in love with the wrong guys?" I asked.

"Oh honey. Come over for the weekend please? I wanna make sure you're okay." She said.

*Her mum thought it was Caleb. She knows about this stalker that wants to kill Ella and she's NOT calling every day to check on her daughter? And she doesn't know about Hunter? He might be just as dangerous as Caleb if you ask me. He's possessive and has angry mood swings. Ella is going to her mother for relationship advice. This would have been a good time to reintroduce Kayla or Lisa or one of the other nurses as a confidant. There are lots of missed opportunities from this ghostwriter...*

"I will mamma I will. I'm coming home." I said and ended the call after a while. Maybe going back home would clear my mind at least. I got ready and went at work. I looked at time. At this time Hunter would just come and visit me for a few hours. More like he came tired and we talked or we just had some fun.

I sighed when I heard a knock on the door. "COME IN." I said and the door opened and Amy, one of the doctors that were working here walked in. "Hey ella you okay?" She asked and I nodded.

"You asked me to come what's up?" She asked. "I uhm I'm going at my parents for the weekend. I hope that's okay." I said and she nodded. "Okay cool. Don't worry everything will go just fine here." She said and I smiled politely.

"Thanks Amy." I said and she chuckled. "No problem. Now I have to go see ya." She said and left my office. I sighed and the door opened once again and I looked up to see Hunter.

*So Ella DOES still work at the hospital and she's summoned Amy to her. Schedules are pretty flexible in a hospital aren't they? She casually says she wants the weekend off and Amy is like – cool! No worries Ella! Whatever you want.*

He slammed the door closed and walked closer. "Why did you leave?" He asked. "Are you joking Hunter?" I said and stood up. "No you were the one that fucking told me we can't keep doing what we were doing. I was okay with that." He said and I shook my head. "Yeah I tell you that and next thing you do is bring a girl at the house I was still in. I heard you guys all night why did you do that?"

"Why did you do that Hunter?" I asked and a tear fell down my face. "Why did you tell me that Ella?" He asked and I let out a sarcastic laugh. "Because all I ever do is fall in love with the wrong guys." I said and he looked at me shocked.

"What?" He said and I walked and opened the door.

"Leave please. Just go." I said and he looked at me.

"Please Hunter let's forget about it and you can go be with that girl whatever her name was." I said and he sighed. "I did that so you could fucking come to me." He said and slammed the door closed again.

"Hunter leave." I said and he shook his head. He then opened the door and left.

*Hunter is ridiculous. He doesn't know WHY Ella left? He has no idea! Really? Then he claims that he only brought that girl (Catherine) home to fuck all night so that Ella would come to him? WHAT? Seriously? What kind of plan is that?*

"What the hell did you wake up from the wrong side of bed " Ian said and I groaned. "Leave me alone." I said.

"Whatever come at the gym quickly." He said and I rolled my eyes and ended the call. I got dressed and I looked at Ella. "I have to go." I said and she smiled. "Okay I'm gonna wait for you at lunch." She said biting her lip and I licked my lips.

I walked closer and kissed her. She kissed me back and then pulled away. "See you later." I said and left.

*Okay WHAT HAS HAPPENED here? They had sex? It feels like there is a scene missing. Ian rang and summoned Hunter to the gym. He's getting dressed and Ella is there. Now – despite their fight – she's waiting for him at lunch? Also this chapter was supposed to be from Ella's point of view. It's hard to tell whose point of view it is. This is jarring which makes the story seem all over the place.*

## CHAPTER TEN

### ELLA'S POINT OF VIEW

I arrived at my hometown and looked outside my parents house. The house were I basically spent my whole life in. I smiled and knocked on the door. The door opened and I saw my mum and I smiled and hugged her.

"Aww my baby I missed you." She said and I smiled. "I missed you too mum." I said pulling away. "Come on in." She said and I walked in.

We walked in the living room where my dad was and I smiled. "Hey dad." I said and he smiled and stood up to hug me. I hugged him back then pulled away. "I missed you my little princess." He said and I smiled and sat down on the couch. "How is work going?" My dad asked and I smiled.

"It's going just fine." I said and he smiled and stood up. "I'm gonna go at work I'll be back earlier though for dinner." He said kissing my head and walking off. My mum took a seat next to me and smiled. "What's wrong honey?" She asked and I sighed.

*The dad calls her princess...Hunter calls her princess... that's kind of creepy. The dad says hi and then leaves right away. He seems super caring doesn't he? He asks Ella about work and then leaves for work. 'Don't forget to make me dinner!' Maybe some of her issues with men can be traced back to her father...*

"I met someone." I said and she smiled waiting for me to continiue. "I met this guy and I just didn't want to feel alone. We had a thing but it wasn't serious and I found myself falling for him." I said and sighed rubbing my face.

"Mum my heart broke for the first time. I always go and fall for the wrong guys." I said and she hugged me. "Honey have you told him?" She asked when I pulled away and sighed. "Sort of. I uhm we lived together for a couple weeks and everything. He was acting so sweet and caring that he made me love him." I said and she sighed.

*Her heart broke for the FIRST time? So Ella chooses the wrong type of guys – Caleb included – and this is the first time shes actually fallen in love with one. Ah! A time frame! They lived together for a couple of weeks! WAS Hunter acting so 'sweet and caring' really? Think about it Ella! He's been a jerk!*

"Ella I think you should talk to him. Tell him what you feel that will make everything better honey." She said and I sighed. "I'm scared. Hunter for sure doesn't feel the same." I said. "Anyways I came here to just clear my mind. Is my room still empty?" I asked and she smiled. "Of course it is honey." She said and I smiled and walked upstairs in my old room.

I closed the door and I looked at my old room. I sat on bed and I found my old books. I chuckled. Such a nerd I was back in high school. I heard my phone and I grabbed it and checked the text.

Hey where are you I'm worried? –Kayla

At least someone was worried about me. I smiled and texted her back.

I'm at my parents I wanted to be a little away from everything you know? Oh hope you feel better soon babe -Kayla

*Tell him how you feel? She did! Ella told Hunter she was falling for him already. Didn't work. Why is Kayla worried? What reason does she have to worry? Why hasn't her Mum asked about Caleb? She seemed concerned on the phone before.*

I sighed and placed the phone on the nightstand and I just laid in bed. After a while I heard the door and I opened my eyes to see my two sisters and my two brothers in my room. "WELCOME HOME ELLA." They screamed and I chuckled and hugged them. " I missed you guys." I said and we walked downstairs. "So any lucky guy in your life?" Jasmine asked and I rolled my eyes playfully.

"No I don't have time." I said and we sat on the dinning table.

My sister Jasmine was the older one from the girl. She was 26 and she was basically gorgeous and had boys drool over her. Sarah was 20 years old and she was still in college. Then my twin brothers Alexander and Benjamin were the youngest one. They were 17 and obviously still in high school. "It's so good to see all my kids in the house." My mum said and I smiled.

"Yeah feels good being back." I said.

*Ella has a pretty big family! Why are we only just learning about this? They sat ON the dining table. Like in the movie Sixteen Candles. What a bunch of details about her siblings. Too little too late though as the story is basically over.*

"HUNTER?" I snapped out of it and I looked at Ian. "What?" I said and he rolled his eyes. "Are you serious? Focus." He said and I threw the gloves away. "Leave me the fuck alone okay? I'm tired I'm leaving." I said and started walking off.

"HUNTER GET BACK HERE." He yelled and I got in my car and hit the steering wheel. I sighed and drove off. I missed Ella. I missed having her around me. I drove at a club and just walked in. Maybe I can take my mind off her.

I walked in and ordered a drink when a girl walked over at me. "Well hello there." She said and I looked at her and smirked. "Hey." I said and he gasped.

"Omg are you Thunder?" She asked and I chuckled. "Of course." I said and she chuckled. "Wow you're even hotter in sight." She said biting her lip.

"Here you go Hunter." The barman said and I nodded. "Thanks." I said and took a sip of the drink. "So wanna have some fun?" She said and I looked at her. She was nothing like Ella though. Her eyes were brown while Ella's eyes were green.

Her hair were blonde but Ella's were just light brown. I sighed and looked down. "I'm sorry." I said and she looked at me confused. "I have to go." I said and walked off. I sighed when I walked out and just got in my car.

I grabbed my phone and looked at Ella's phone number. I called Ella and waited for her to pick it up. When she didn't answer I sighed and placed the phone down. I'm tired. I've been thinking of her all day all night every second.

She's driving me crazy. I've never thought of a girl before. All I ever do is fuck and run. This is just stressing me out.

*Here we are featuring Hunter's point of view in an Ella chapter yet again. Another random girl recognises him as Thunder and says 'omg' AGAIN. It's so repetitive. The way he compares the physical traits of this new woman and Ella is disturbing. He's never THOUGHT of a girl before? Is he a serial killer? Oh boy... I'm glad this one is over. Hunter's so unlikable. It's stressing YOU out to have feelings is it? She has a crazy stalker! Ella is the one that should be stressed. But you keep moping.*

Ten chapters of poorly compiled rubbish. On the whole this felt like a pre-written template that the second ghostwriter manipulated – poorly – to suit my needs. Ella and Hunter were probably substituted for whatever names were in there the last time the template was used. Maybe that's why Ozan, Zayn, John, Oliver, Amy and Bels were still in there. They could have been leftover characters from the previous re-write or the last writer's story.

It didn't feel personally tailored to me and it wasn't really what I'd asked for. It was about a sex-crazed guy and included a subplot about a stalker. I guess I had hoped for something funnier. I wanted a continuation of the first ghostwriter's work. It didn't gel together at all. These characters were not the same as *The Hunter* and *Obsession*. Ella had no interest in wrestling and the ten thousand words barely featured any at all.

## PART THREE

It was time to bring the *Dropping the Belt* experiment to an end. But how exactly? The story parts weren't fitting together like I'd hoped they would. It wasn't really about wrestling anymore. It was hard to incorporate any ideas from the second ghostwriter as she missed the mark so completely. Reading it again made me feel even more certain that this delivery was a template that had been customised to fit my story. This wasn't original at all.

I should have seen it when the second ghostwriter didn't have any follow up questions. Why did it take her a week to complete then? She only needed to change the character names. By her own admission she wasn't working on anything else. There were so many characters that made no sense within the story. Who were all the males that Hunter was with at the start? Who was Thunder for that matter?! She hadn't understood what I was after at all and that annoyed me. The first part of the story was entertaining. This nonsense was full of nodding, sighing, groaning and raising eyebrows.

For the record here is a count of how many times these actions were performed:

| | |
|---|---|
| NODDED | 26 |
| SMILED | 19 |
| SIGHING | 18 |
| CHUCKLED | 14 |
| RAISING EYEBROW | 8 |
| GIGGLING | 7 |
| GROANING | 6 |
| MOANING | 6 |
| SMIRKING | 6 |

If *Dropping the Belt* was to be a trilogy I'd need a strong final act. I started chatting to a third ghostwriter about concluding the story despite the off brand nature of the second part. I found a willing ghostwriter that boasted about his writing and translating skills on his profile. I asked him how much it would be to write the required ten thousand words. He replied briefly with: 'Not much.' After some discussion about the themes and ideas of my story he agreed to write ten thousand words for the price of $35. After I had booked his services for the third part and the money had changed hands the ghostwriter was in touch again.

GHOSTWRITER #3:

Hello dear friend I have an advice for this.

ME:

What is your advice?

GHOSTWRITER #3:

Above 2k or 3k words will be nonsense. If you want this look short brave and sweet make it 2000 words.

I told him I disagreed. At this point I reiterated all of the story points that I wanted him to tell beat by beat. I finished by stating 'once you start writing it will end up as more words that you think.'

GHOSTWRITER #3:

Okay because I'm possible entering into the page of Ella so was thinking will not be okay. Okay as a creative writer let me do my job.

The language barrier sometimes makes people seem ruder than they are. I wasn't taking his blunt words personally. After the allocated week he delivered only 2500 words and I confronted him about it. He stressed that it was 'fine' and that he had shown it to five different writers and they 'confirm that it was a really great story from the beginning to the ending.' I didn't believe he had shown it to five writers.

In his story the characters barely spoke at all. I asked for more dialogue and he said he would work on it. Within 24 hours he delivered an additional 1500 words and said that he 'discovered it was okay like that. Just perfect.'

I told him I would give him more time to write but he asked for more money. He told me I'd worked him 'like a slave' and told me that writing the full ten thousand words was a 'suicide mission' for him. He told me I wouldn't find any ghostwriter that would write ten thousand words so cheaply despite the fact I already had – twice! I agree that the price was low. I probably wouldn't have carried out this experiment if it was cost prohibitive.

Ghostwriter #3 was annoyed about the price that he had agreed to and in a snarky message to me he said that the 4000 words he delivered were so good that 'even William Shakespear will rate me %100 for the creativity.' All spelling mistakes have been left in as always.

Well dear reader… in Mr Shakespeare's absence I will ask you to read the 4000 words and judge for yourself. I have had to manually insert breaks in which to add my own *italic* notes as the story was delivered in one massive paragraph.

Enjoy.

In about the early 90s there was a very young successful young man by name Hunter who live all his life to love an endures wrestling, so he when in for trainings so as to be as a wrestler too. All in a sudden he became one or the most successful trainee in his camp. So here step his first travel to India where is was well snack down by top warriors in India so the fight was schedule in two weeks time. So Hunter when back to his coach and was well trained again where he took some order good training from a top old and best wrestler from Australia who saw success in this handsome young man's eyes so decided to sponsor his training a week and some days .So Hunter was now ready for the next fight still in India, why on the battle field the Indian wrestler thought Hunter was still the first Hunter they knew,. So there goes the bell jingling ring ring first round start said by the referee and the fight started, Noting that this fight was scheduled for thirty minute ( 30 minutes ) unfortunately Hunter took just fifteen minute ( 15 Minutes ) to but this man down,.

*Here we go again! Hunter is a professional wrestler that is travelling the world. He's described in the opening line as 'very young' and 'young' so we might as well imagine a small child. He gets 'smacked down' (which is what I assume 'snack down' translates to) which means Hunter gets defeated while he's in India. I'm not sure what fight is being scheduled. People look at him and see a future winner! It's so difficult for me to ignore the spelling mistakes and incorrect words – but I'll try! Who was the FIRST Hunter they knew? I don't understand that. I want to ignore the language barrier but how do you ignore the phrase 'so there goes the bell jingling ring ring?' Isn't it 'unfortunate' that he won in half the required time? Don't you hate it when that happens? Obviously this third ghostwriter has their own unique style...*

It was really surprising but for Hunter, the game just started and for such handsome young man so many women started to go close to him thou Hunter was a very shy handsome young guy so he was always afraid of women each time they came close to him. So as time goes by Hunter left India for United state Of America where he was forced to fight a closed cage fight thou he lamented and was well tutored but Hunter was still very determined to win this fight., In about a few minutes of the second fight ( $2^{nd}$ fight ) round Hunter thought of his lovely family washing him back home why he is being tutored so he pickup the challenge once more thou still believing in his self and with the courage and love towards his wrestling game he end up wining the deadly cage fight so again and again Hunter became the undefeated Wrestler of the that year

*Okay so women are interested in Hunter but he's shy. This ghostwriter has also misunderstood the kind of wrestling I wanted in this story. That makes three out of three! Maybe I'm the problem? They have him travelling the world and fighting in cages. Professional wrestling doesn't traditionally have cages (unless it's a cage match) nor does it have rounds. Hunter thought of his family... 'washing' him... back home? Huh? Oh he probably means WATCHING. Geez. That's a bad word to get wrong. He's undefeated is he? I thought he was 'smacked down' in India. Fine, so by believing in himself and remembering his loved ones he won the fight.*

So I another year came and Hunter was still the man of the year thou he wasn't good enough in cage fighting so Hunter  United State Of America for Russia where he when into another training but that was different from the order training he used to have in the previous countries .Why in Russia Hunter when clubbing one night with friends and saw a girls were he was seduced but he wasn't in love because Hunter's best music artist then was Ed Sheeran and in he loves and always listen to this particular music 'Shape of you' thou the next morning Hunter wanted to go back to this place for breakfast because of this same girls but he had no time because he was to go down to Moscow for another cage training lessons and back then Hunter could do any thing in order to keep in touch with his training so he definitely left for Moscow.

*Hunter's the 'man of the year' now. Like Time Magazine's Man of the Year? Okay he's moved to Russia and overcome his shyness towards women. In fact he's out clubbing! Hunter met a girl but didn't fall in love. It sounds like he spent the night with her though. Ed Sheeran is his favourite artist? In the 90's? Ed Sheeran was BORN in 1991! The song 'Shape of You' didn't come out until 2017. Maybe Hunter was just waaaaay ahead of his time in his musical tastes.*

After and hour or two Hunter saw a very nice looking young girl by name Ella thou she was also shy from guys but was always determined to do what so ever it takes for her to do just to be a wrestler thou Ella was looking at Hunter like someone who does not even know how to look in to any wrestler's eyes mean why on the order hand Hunter was busily admiring Ella's training skills thou then Ella was not that strong enough to be called a wrestler but one thing Hunter loves about Ella thou just looking into Ella's eyes was, she was very determined to do anything it will take to be a top female wrestler just as Hunter was some few years back.

*Alright. I'll give this third ghostwriter some credit for actually having Ella want to be a professional wrestler. She was looking at Hunter like 'someone who does not even know how to look in to any wrestler's eyes'? What does THAT mean?*

*They are staring at eachother from across the training rooms. I don't know if she likes him AT ALL. And the writer calls her weak. That's a bit harsh.*

As it goes Hunter happens to meet with Ella on a morning trained up at the gym since Ella was a very shy young lady as well as Hunter so it both took a very long time for both to come or talk together but deeply in Ella's mind she was still falling for Hunter and as a young determined girl so she never wanted to make it look like she was so cheap or some think like that so she keeps running away from Hunter and as time goes by for Hunter he had just one month ( 1 month ) and a few weeks in Russia facing the fact that Hunter had to be on continues training because he was about to face some warriors in Hon Kong and time was running so fast for Hunter to arrange for a date out with Ella.

*They are both super shy – although I thought Hunter got over that when he was clubbing? Ella's falling for him but doesn't want to be viewed as cheap. So she runs away from him? I don't know why the ghostwriter is putting things in brackets like that. Now we are going to Hong Kong. Alright... Tell me who is paying for all of these crazy international flights and accommodation? The Australian 'sponsor' that believed in him at the start?*

But God being to kind on Hunter's which was the morning his flight was schedule shift and draft the next morning due to Moscow bad weather, so that night at the wrestling bank there was a chair and on the chair they was a lady sitting lonely on it and thou Hunter never could imagine it was Ella so Hunter batch up to the lady to find out what's wrong with her but to his grate surprise it was Ella so Hunter comforted Ella for Ella explained to him how she lost her dad in plane crash why going to United Kingdom for a business trip so Hunter also told Ella how he lost his dad too because he was seriously ill then their family could not afford for his father's hospitals bills so they where chase out of the hospital because of that so Hunter told Ella how he himself watch his father die on his mom's arms just because they never had money to take good care of him and as a matter of fact Ella with a very week heart as a woman started crying and Hunter had to look into Ella's eyes to tell her that all what happen was in the pass so here comes the feature so she should not be thinking about stories anymore…

*So it was God that caused the bad weather and allowed them to see eachother again… at the wrestling 'bank'? The lonely lady on a chair WAS Ella! They are bonding over the fact that neither of them has a father anymore. Hunter's family was chased out of the hospital! What a visual. And poor 'week' Ella with her womanly heart! She starts crying because she's a woman and that's what women do, right? 'Here comes the feature' is obviously 'here comes the future' but I like it better the way he writes it.*

…and that same moment Hunter started kissing Ella but before he could notice it was already morning so he had to take a flight for his wrestling game in Hong Kong so he had no choice than to allow Ella and get going for what he has always dreamed of thou one think Hunter forgot to do was he never took Ella's Cell phone number so there was really no way for him to get in contact with Ella due to the mistake he made thou was not his fault at all .Mean why on the order hand Hunter was in the plane but his mind could not stop thinking of Ella so he was looking worried but he never told his coach about his feelings for Ella thou his coach already saw it in his eyes before they could notice the flight attendant came in telling them the plane will soon be on land so Hunter's coach started talking and giving some fighting tactics so Hunter quickly abide to his coach advice despite the fact that he could not stop thinking of Ella.

*They kissed ALL NIGHT. I wonder why the word 'match' as in wrestling match has been corrected to 'game' by this ghostwriter. Hunter's leaving the girl behind to chase his dream. How was it 'not his fault at all' for not getting her number? Whose fault was it? He's distracted now. He's thinking about Ella and their kiss.*

knock knock at the plane alert here comes the flight attendant ladies and gentlemen thank for your patient and we all thank the almighty God for flying us to Hong Kong safely, Hunter's coach step down the plane step and directly behind him was Hunter and the most amazing was Hunter never knew he had fans in Hong Kong as well, . When the coach look at the crowed made of too many young youth and their parents too cheering for Hunter so Hunter's coach look at it as a blessing and decided to visit the radio house that same night so that Hunter could give some advice to the youth out the street of Hong Kong and parents as well .

*'Knock knock' at the plane alert? Geez. That's hard to take. Sorry dear reader. I guess that's an announcement on the plane? But 'knock knock' is a rough way to write a 'ding' sound effect. The flight attendants are pushing their heavily religious views onto the patrons. Hunter has fans in Hong Kong. The crowd at the airport waiting for them is made up of too many 'young youths' so they decide to go to the 'radio house' and address them all at once. Why is it a big deal if it's many 'young youths' anyway? I suppose this means Hunter is a role model – but isn't that considered a good thing? They love wrestlers in Hong Kong I guess.*

It is 6 pm Hong Kong time here and here we have Mr, Alfred the number on ( 1 ) world best coach and his boy here by name Hunter so the radio man handed over the microphone to Mr, Alfred to say a few words and people thought Mr, Alfred was going to be boost of himself but instead Mr, Alfred just gave a very short and intelligent speech

*Okay so this is the radio announcer talking? Mr Alfred is the number one 'world's best coach' is he? You know it's a professional radio show when the announcer is handing the only microphone to his guest. Here comes the short speech I suppose.*

' Ladies and Gentlemen I thank you all for giving me your ears to hear to me I know so well that you guys are expecting me to say something long and expensive but rather I'm going to give this little advice to the youth that be determined in what so ever you want to do, put more consideration on it and never forget to pray for more strength because we only wish and God makes the wish true depending on how determined you are and Mr, Alfred concluded thanks and please youth do not take this short advice for granted once more thank you guys so much so now you can hear from Hunter your wrestler thou people were expecting that Mr, Alfred should address Hunter as a warrior instead he said your wrestler ,Hunter' in addition to what my father, coach, promoter and best friend already said please dear youth believe in yourself and make sure you never get faith up when thinks seems not to be moving well but rather increase your man power toward what so ever you have in mind and again I will also tell you guys to listen and also take advice to your parents because they are the only friends on earth that will never mean bad or evil on each of you all, thank you all once more and see you tomorrow evening at the arena and I pray each and every one of you be a blessing to your families concluded by saying amen…

*I've had to break in again…the thing that really stands out for me here is that in the previous section Hunter is referred to as Mr Alfred's 'boy' and in this section Hunter says his coach is his father. His father DIED because they were poor. It was the reason he and Ella bonded. This is all very religious. I wonder if the ghostwriter always includes God in his writing. I don't know about all this 'wishing' business. You can't just wish to be a good fighter and then be one. He should be preaching that the youth need to work hard to reach their goals. Also WHY do people expect the coach to refer to him as a warrior and not a wrestler? He's a wrestler. I love the phrase 'increase your man power' in this speech. There is a whole bunch of generalising here when it comes to parents. Some parents are shitty. You can't just give the youth of Hong Kong these blanket statements Hunter!*

…and the microphone was handed back to the radio man ( Journalise ) and the journalise was confused so wanted to ask more questions to Mr, Alfred about hunter but Mr, Alfred did turn down all request of asking any more question that his boy is tired and need some rest for the next day evening match so Hunter when back to his rest room thou cannot still stop thinking of still take out the memories of Ella's kiss in his mind which seems to be Hunter's point of consideration and at the same time a distraction too because Hong Kong wrestlers where not so easy as coach Alfred could think. Knock Knock at Hunter's door and he answer please who is they come in and the person who came in was coach Alfred and he told Hunter to believe in his self no matter if he is having less fans or no fans at all and the worst part of it was coach Alfred told Hunter why on his way out was 'always remember that your kid ones at home ( siblings ) are watching at you not living out Ella too and again coach saw some courage in Hunter like never before .

*So the 'radio man' wanted to ask a few questions – you know like a radio interview – and they acted like jerks. Ella is definitely a distraction and as we all know Hong Kong wrestlers are not as easy as we think! Except that it's supposed to be fake professional wrestling with a pre-determined outcome. Why is his father/coach coming to his room before a big fight to tell him 'even if he has no fans' to believe in himself? We KNOW Hunter has fans! They were there when the plane landed. That's why you went to the radio station – remember? He has siblings? Are they living in poverty? Does he send money home to them? So many questions...*

Bouncing at the Arena was one of the Hong Kong best wrestler and all Hunter could hear was people hailing at him and on the order part comes Hunter and Hunter's fans began hailing at him thou they were not too much at compared to those of his opponent even thou that does not give enough reason that his opponent was going to win but on his opponent mind he knew he was just going to kill Hunter because Hunter was not that huge as compared to him so many people in the hall knew Hunter was going to be tortured like a kid.

*'Bouncing' at the arena? I think this is meant to mean that his opponent was bouncing around the ring. Who is his opponent? Oh it's one of Hong Kong's best wrestlers. But who is he? Don't overthink it... he's just one of the best. Are they chanting his name? Yes! What is his name? Um... don't know! I'm glad he recognises that the loudest chant doesn't determine the winner. His opponent wants to 'kill' Hunter and 'torture him' like a KID? WHAT? Who tortures kids?*

Here comes the first round of the wrestling battle ( $1^{st}$ round ) and Hunter was well beaten but for him he was trying to study the opponent wrestling skills so it happen he was beaten mysteriously, so the opponent thought things were going to be the same as the first round ( $1^{st}$ round ) of fight but unfortunately it was different for him because Hunter was not the same Hunter he thought again because the first 2 minutes of the second round ( $2^{nd}$ round ) he was snack down and the referee counted up to five ( 5 ) but the opponent could not wakeup again and the bells jingles and fans began to hail at Hunter and the referee confirm that Hunter was the winner of the game. It ended for Hunter that day as one of the most successful wrestler so another fight was scheduled after two weeks ( 2 weeks ).

*I think – because of the rounds – that this writer has confused professional wrestling with UFC. Maybe that's why opponents are trying to kill each other. He was beaten 'mysteriously' in the first round? Like it was a surprise? It doesn't sound like a surprise because his opponent is bigger and more popular than him. And as we know Hong Kong fighters shouldn't be underestimated.*

For Hunter he was happy to go back to Moscow ( Russia ) so that he could meet up with Ella once more time but unfortunately the time he was supposed to take a flight back to Moscow his coach decided to put him on intense training because he already knew the next wrestling game is going to be a cage wrestling fight thou he knew Hunter was not that good and cage fight so Hunter used two weeks (2 weeks) to train like a slave just because he was to face one of the world most dangerous wrestling game fight ever thou Hunter was not afraid at all to face the beast in the cage because he knew if he succeeded from the cage fight he was going to be a top snack down wrestler so Hunter thought of it being as a point of courage for Ella to keep up with her trainings and it goes on for some week and some days that Hunter has been training thou on was already a top news that Hunter was going to be the top fighter in the history of snack down wrestling .

*Hunter's fighting every two weeks? I feel like even UFC events are monthly at the earliest. This feels like an excessive training regime AND excessive fighting schedule. Hunter WON the last cage fight. So he IS good at cage fights. How does one train 'like a slave' anyway? Build a pyramid? Is he fighting a 'wrestling game' fighter or a 'beast' next? Or is his next opponent named The Beast? If he wins he'll be a top 'smackdown' wrestler. Smackdown is one of the more famous WWE televised programs. So this is even more convoluted. The news are reporting that he will be the best in 'history' though so I guess success is in Hunter's future.*

Now the day finally comes fans hailing at Hunter in the cage so the fight began to the greatest surprised ever the fight when for up to five rounds ( 5 rounds ) but the sixth round was not an easy one for Hunter for he was injured seriously in such a way when Hunter was taken to the hospital the Doctor told him that might be the end of his carrier thou Hunter was known worldwide for his brave wrestling battles. So Hunter left Hong Kong for Moscow just because of Ella thou still sustaining injury but with love and care toward Ella he had to teach Ella how to wrestle and God so good Ella was picking up and so love  continues being in between them so Ella had keep living with Hunter so that she could be taking care of Hunter and it was well known that they were already engage and they both plan to make a white wedding in Australia  and Ella had to live for Australia as soon as possible living Hunter behind to meet her after so all when well for the both of them for and a day was set for Ella's flight to Australia and the day finally came so Hunter had to go see Ella at the airport and they both departed only to see in a few weeks again and all they did was talk all night until one of their phone will finally be battery low or something will happen like either of them fallen to sleep.

*Wow. Quite a fall from grace for Hunter. He's on top of the wrestling world and then just like that he might never wrestle again. So Hunter is injured but he's training Ella in Moscow now? And surprise! They are also engaged. That was fast… and I really enjoyed the detail… I feel like I was THERE you know? Why are they getting married in Australia? That has definitely not been explained. Is that Australian sponsor from earlier paying for their wedding too? Very confusing. Ella was leaving without him, then they both 'departed' and then they would see each other in a few weeks. Luckily they can talk on the phone. Say… how cheap were international phone calls between Moscow and Australia in the 90's? So cheap that you could talk all night and fall asleep on the phone. What a time it was…*

This is how Hunter's whole live ended thou falling in love seriously with Ella. Since Ella was already in Australia with Hunter's parents, so she decided to continue her trainings and unfortunately the Australian Government hosted a female tournament wrestling games and Ella was so excited going in for it thou Hunter's parents where against it because they never wanted what happened to Hunter to happen to their son's wife but Ella insisted up to an extend that she had to call Hunter and ask for permeation from him since she really loves Hunter so much and never wanted to go against his rolls ( wish ) and with the sweet roses from Ella's voice, Hunter was charmed by the voice and decided to allow Ella go in for the Australian female wrestling's games thou for Hunter he knew Ella was a woman of prediction and determination and more to that he was one hundred percent ( 100% ) sure that Ella will make it in the games.

*Sorry… his whole LIFE ended? So he's dead? Sorry again… Ella's in Australia with Hunter's parents? His father – who died because they were poor – and his mother? Where are the siblings that were mentioned earlier? Inconsistent!*

*Sorry...and maybe it's just me...but I think he's using the word 'unfortunately' wrong again. It is a good thing (not an unfortunate one) that the Australian Government put on a wrestling tournament. It would absolutely NEVER happen. Nobody would be happy about their taxes funding this nonsense. I guess they got married then? Ella's his 'wife' now. She still has to ask his permission to enter though. And she has to use the 'sweet roses' of her voice to convince Hunter.*

The following day Ella called Hunter and confess to Hunter how much she loves him and will do what so ever it takes to make him proud once more again and Hunter was warmed-hearted and also promise Ella how he is going to do what so ever it takes for her to win the games and make her mamma a proud woman for ever, why they were discussing Hunter's mother came in and over heard them promising and telling each order how much they love each order and she also heard how Hunter told Ella how much he knows she will be the top at the games. After the call Hunter's mother called Ella and ask her if they could take a walk together and she was so impressed and she never waited for Hunter's mother to finish talking but she already accepted.

*So Ella forgot to tell him she loves him during their previous call? Also what is HE going to do to make sure she wins the games? Hunter's in Moscow isn't he? There is nothing he can do. So what on Earth is going on here? Hunter's mother – who Ella is staying with – asks her to come for a walk. Ella is so impressed that she would even ASK to take a walk? Huh?*

So as they were take a walk down the street Hunter's mother thought of a cold tree at the river side where she and her husband ( Hunter's father ) used to seat they before he passed out and she never hesitated to take Ella to the river side meanwhile at the riverside she told Ella how she and Hunter's father used to seat they the whole day and promised never to live each order after saying all this she started crying thou when Ella told her to stop crying she said I'm not crying of the old memory but I'm cry and wishing if my husband ( Hunter's father ) was still alive to see how love rolls in you both and at that same riverside she gave Ella a golden necklace which given to her by her mother before she passed out too and she told Ella why giving the necklace that it is a necklace of love and success she should handle it with care because she is the mother of the family considering the fact that Hunter's mother was already an old woman and Ella receives the necklace with too much respect and love and also promise Hunter's mother that she will make sure everything is okay in their family...

*The mother 'thought' of a cold tree? Okay... and it seems like the ghostwriter has remembered that Hunter's father 'passed out' which probably means 'passed away.' Hunter's parents used to sit at the riverside and promise one another that they would never leave? Her mother gave her a golden necklace before she passed away – or passed out. Then we have a dig at Hunter's mother being super old.*

...so it was too cold and they left to the house and Ella could not stop adoring the necklace so she called Hunter and told Hunter how she and his mother enjoyed the day by the riverside so and Hunter was so impress and could not wait to see her queen in the fighting arena the next day. Since it was already late in the night Ella when to bed hoping to wake up early but all in a sudden she woke up very late that she was almost cancel as one of the candidates wrestling for that year, Ella never knew Hunter already hired one of the best female coach for her thou she only discover when she was at the arena and a lady came up and ask her to sign and contract of accepting her as her coach so Ella was confused because it was not a day then to hire that particular woman as a coach no matter how much you can offer her so Ella sign the contract and immediately she sign the contract...

*Is Hunter flying back to watch her fight? Or is he watching from Moscow? We don't know what kind of injury he has sustained. Maybe he can't travel at all. Ella overslept and almost missed being a 'candidate' for the tournament. It's odd that Hunter hired her a 'female' coach. It's all wrestling and you would think there wouldn't be a gender distinction. Also wasn't HIS coach the number one best coach ever? Shouldn't he have hired his father/coach Mr. Alfred to train Ella? The new female coach brought the contract to the arena. That's a ballsy move isn't it? What if Ella had said no?*

...she was directed to her dressing but when she get to the room for her to get dressed and be set for the fight she instead took the time to call Hunter to tell him how much he meant to her whole life and carrier too before she could noticed her coach batch in and yield at with a very strong voice because she was a lady who does not jokes when it comes to time so Ella rushly dressed up and step outside all she could hear was her name mixed with Hunter's name, so many people were shouting Hunter-Ella Hunter-Ella so she was just too happy and impressed .

*She's super distracted by Hunter too. They can't stop distracting eachother. Couldn't Ella have made this phone call BEFORE this moment? And now she's calling Moscow from the phone in the arena because mobile phones aren't that common yet. The coach is mad about the time now that Ella is her client. She wasn't mad earlier when she nearly missed the whole competition because she slept in! People are chanting for her and Hunter? So she's also a celebrity now?*

The bell jingles and she entered the arena thou with all the treat the opponent came close to her and told her she will make sure Ella does not goes home with all her two legs but to the greatest surprised Ella tottered her opponent almost to dead thou the referee divided the fight and ask the opponent if she could continue the fight again but she refused and gave up and Ella was announced the winner and she was so so happy and her next match was already finals, since it was just within Australia so there weren't too many fixtures and when Hunter heard of her brave did at the arena so he decided to come to book a flight immediately to Australia but Ella's coach told Hunter not to come too early so they plan that he will arrive that same day of Ella's finals.

*The bell jingles… Merry Christmas I guess. Her opponent's threat was to make sure she didn't leave with 'all her two legs.' So she's planning on removing one – or some – of her legs? And the Australian Government is sanctioning this? Ella 'tottered' her opponent 'almost to dead' too. Why is her coach determining Hunter's travel plans? Why does she get a say? She only just got hired. Is she paying for the flights? And if Ella had lost just now when WAS Hunter coming back to Australia? Shouldn't he have been there for the fight? It's kind of an important moment for his wife.*

As time goes by they kept talking over the phone and Ella by mistakenly mention that she wish if Hunter could be by her on the final's day thou not knowing that Hunter already plan it that he will surprise Ella why Ella in already inside the arena ready for the fight . Now comes the day when Ella had to go in for the final game meanwhile Hunter was already in Australia but decided to spend the night with his friend till when it was time. So Hunter decided to sleep so that he could have some energy at the hall where the fight was scheduled .

*They keep running up that phone bill. So Hunter coming to see her is a surprise? Then truly – why did he run it by her coach first? And then when he gets to Australia he's spending the night with a friend? That sounds like an affair to me. Isn't he rich? Wouldn't he stay in a hotel? No. He WANTS to stay with that friend.*

When was already time and Ella was already in the arena waiting for the opponent and the opponent came thou she looked weaker than the previous person she fought but her coach told her it does not matter all matters is what the person (opponent ) is capable of doing so the bell jingles and the fight started and as time goes it getting more stronger than Ella thought . In this fight Ella was beaten like a one year ( 1 year ) old baby despite all her trainings and the worst part of it was she was almost giving up till when she saw Hunter and could not believe it was Hunter but Hunter came close and talk to her about her promises and once more again Ella gain some strain and open a good attack on her opponent and before she could discover Ella was already winning the fight and it came to a point that her opponent had to give up because she has been tortured just as did earlier to Ella but should not take the pains again and she final gave up and the referee announces Ella as the winner of the game but for Ella the game was nothing to her all that matters then to her was to hold Hunter one more time after a long while
So Ella left the field with Hunter home and they were both happy and love keep flowing in their means.

*Don't judge your opponent by how weak they look. That's good advice because on this occasion Ella is 'beaten like a one year old baby' by her opponent. Jeez! This is a horrible visual. Then – in her beaten state – she sees Hunter. Why didn't he reveal himself to her earlier than this? He came 'close' to talk to her? I'm assuming he did this between rounds and not just while Ella was in a headlock.*

*Ella wins the match (Game? Tournament? Who knows!) but it doesn't matter to her. All she wanted to do was be with Hunter. Did she give up wrestling to be with him? Ella won...so she got some prize money or something? There are so few details here that I couldn't tell you whether she's through to the next round or if she's won the whole thing.*

What you have just read is almost four thousand words. I had requested ten thousand to match with the previous two writers. Would 'Shakespear' have loved those words? I can't speak for the Bard but I found them challenging. At least they felt as though they were written for me and my story. This wasn't a pre-written template of work but it was pretty terrible. The divide in language is evident from beginning to end.

This entire transaction left me feeling like the project *still* wasn't over.

## PART FOUR

With the short and ultimately disappointing delivery from the third ghostwriter the story wasn't as conclusive as I wanted it to be. It was becoming a frustrating experiment. At first I thought I was investing in the wrong ghostwriters. Maybe I just needed one more attempt to get the ending right? I hired one that claimed they were actually a 'collective' of ghostwriters and that I would be receiving the best work from a whole team of writers. The profile image that this collective had chosen was of a girl of about ten years of age. I booked them to conclude the story of Hunter and Ella and after four days I was advised by the website administrator that they were no longer on the site. Were they ripping people off? Plagiarising work? I'll never know why they were reported and blacklisted.

I took the refunded money and booked yet another ghostwriter. I took my time explaining the characters and made sure they knew exactly what kind of professional wrestling I wanted them to write about. I made sure they understood the relationship between Hunter and Ella in painstaking detail. I pitched them the story of an older Hunter being summoned back into the world of professional wrestling with one final lucrative payday. I went back and forth with the writer and made sure they understood what I wanted over several weeks worth of correspondence. They asked me to 'leave the creativeness' to them in a similar manner to the third ghostwriter. I was cautious but proceeded with them nonetheless. I had made sure they had all the information. I had done my best to prepare them. I wanted a conclusion to the story of Hunter and Ella.

They delivered a document that was almost twenty thousand words long. I'd only paid for ten thousand and this was a surprising result.

Unfortunately they missed the mark by a country mile. The story was also titled *Ecstasy of the Heart*. That was weird! Why did they choose *exactly* the same title as the second ghostwriter?

Was there a database of generic titles that they were choosing from? Were there only a handful of writing templates that they simply adjusted to suit the wants of the buyer? It felt dodgy. The experiment was losing its lustre rapidly.

I asked the writer why they chose that particular title. He replied with the word: 'Nothing.' I wasn't able to get any real reason from them. The content of the twenty thousand words was unusable. The ghostwriter had included a disclaimer at the beginning that stated the writing was a 'work of fiction' and that any 'resemblance to actual persons, living or dead' was purely coincidental.

The writer had then delivered a marathon of WWE fan fiction. They included as many current WWE wrestling superstars as they could Google. They wrote out a series of actual moves that the wrestlers were known for. They plagiarised several months worth of storylines that played out during televised WWE events. The main character *was* Hunter but Ella was completely missing from the story. It wasn't what I asked for at all. It was match after match of wrestling without much of a story inbetween. There was ONLY wrestling. It was basically rubbish and I'll spare you from reading it here. It was a complete waste of time and money.

The only remotely interesting part was that the ghostwriter created a finishing move named *Hunter's Rush* but never described it in any detail. Suffice to say I'd learned that with each ghostwriter I engaged to write for me I would never get the result I wanted. You really never knew what you would get. It was like rolling dice. Each of the delivered pieces were so different but still universally bad.

The first writer was unintentionally amusing but didn't understand the rules of professional wrestling. They constructed a relationship that was full of poor decisions from both parties. Ella quit her job to be a valet for crying out loud!

The second writer (I believe) had a template and delivered a story that wasn't really about wrestling at all. The characters were unlikable and nodded at everything they said to one another. Everything about it felt forced. Ella walked everywhere and Hunter was a sex addict.

The third writer wrote something that missed the mark in length, quality and focus. It was as if they typed as quickly as they could and never rewrote their words. The barrier in language resulted in some off putting visuals as well.

The two additional attempts to have someone else write my story had resulted in a cancelled job without explanation and twenty thousand words that felt like WWE fan fiction. It wasn't working anymore. Ghostwriters could no longer assist me with *Dropping the Belt*.

This final part of the story – the Epilogue - was written by me. I have taken cues from the previous stories and attempted to tie up some of the loose ends. In the spirit of this experiment I allowed myself only one week to churn out the six thousand words that were never delivered by the third ghostwriter.

This will conclude the tale of Hunter and Ella once and for all.

## EPILOGUE

The room was cavernous and adorned with trophies and large photographs. Everything had been carefully curated, making it feel more like a museum exhibition than a living room. The most prominent picture, the one that hung over the unused fireplace, was of a couple in their early thirties. They were both smiling and staring straight ahead. The muscular man was shirtless and wore leopard print leggings. The woman in the image was dressed in tight black leather. The photograph was taken at the conclusion of a professional wrestling match. There were beads of sweat running down the man's face but they both looked elated.

Hunter and Ella interlocked their fingers. Their romance had been quite a winding journey. Now they were finally able to sit down and appreciate everything they had been through to get to this moment. The photograph represented a relic from a bygone era of their lives. The couple, though now in their sixties, were still in amazing physical condition. If it weren't for a few visible scars one might not have ever guessed the two had been wrestlers. Hunter's hair was short and grey but it had barely receded. He had a scruff of facial hair and a well-defined chin. Ella had become fuller but still had the same vibrant smile as the girl in the photograph.

The man in the spectacles set up his recording device on the table. He was dressed in a tidy jacket and vest combination and seemed a little bit intimidated by the couple sitting opposite him. He gave a brief smile and took out a notepad from his bag. He turned the recorder on and the interview commenced.
'So let's start at the beginning. How did you two meet?'
Ella smiled and tightened her grip. Hunter's hands might have once resembled those of a piano player but now were rough and calloused.

'Well…I was at my friend Amanda's hen's night and Hunter was one of the topless waiters.'

'Oh wow. That sounds like a memorable night,' said the man.

'You have no idea. Off the record?'

The man nodded his encouragement.

'Amanda and some of my friends were actually *experimenting* with some of the male entertainers.'

'Whoa!'

The interviewer was clearly surprised but Ella decided not to go into any more detail. She could tell that the images he was creating in his head were sufficiently scandalous.

'Amanda is actually dating a former male stripper now,' said Ella with a cheeky smirk.

'You never told me that,' replied Hunter. 'I thought she was still married.'

'Nope. They've been divorced for a while. It's a funny story…'

The man adjusted his glasses with his index finger.

'Sorry to interrupt guys…this is interesting stuff but if we could keep the focus on the two of you? I'm under the pump I'm afraid. The publishers want me to get them the first ten thousand words of your story by the end of the week,' he explained.

'A week is not a lot of time,' mused Hunter.

'No it's not.'

'Have you ever ghostwritten a biography before? It was Dave… wasn't it?' asked Hunter.

Dave nodded.

'This is new to me, actually. It's all a bit daunting.'

'We'd better stay on track for you then,' said Ella with a smile.

'That would be great. Thank you both for making the time today,' he said.

'No problem,' replied Hunter.

Dave noted that Ella seemed completely smitten with her husband. Hunter was very charming and likeable. Dave couldn't wait to get started on their story.

He had been writing for years but this assignment was the biggest yet. Hunter was a celebrity and there had been ongoing demand for a tell-all book. He couldn't believe his luck when he was tasked with the job. He'd been a fan of professional wrestling in his youth, which his employers knew, and that may have contributed to him getting the gig over some of the other writers. He had a lot to prove to the publishers and to himself. Dave hoped to make Hunter and Ella happy too.

'So you met at a hen's party?'

Ella lit up like a Christmas tree.

'We certainly did! Do you want to tell him what you were *wearing* Hunter?' she teased.

Hunter rolled his eyes.

'Look...it was a long time ago and it was my first time as a topless waiter. I didn't realise that you were allowed to wear pants.'

'So what *were* you wearing?' asked Dave as he leaned forward in his chair.

'A thong,' replied Hunter with a sigh.

Ella and Dave laughed together as Hunter nodded to himself. This anecdote had been a constant source of amusement for Ella over the years. Hunter was used to this reaction from his wife.

'You were drinking alot that night Ella, maybe you're remembering it wrong.'

'Oh Hunter it's hard to get that image of you out of my head actually!' replied Ella.

'And is that photograph on the wall here somewhere?' joked Dave, looking around.

'Unfortunately...or should I say *fortunately* nobody had a camera that night,' said Hunter.

'Well, let's start there,' said Dave. 'What were your first impressions of Hunter?' Ella placed a hand on Hunter's knee as she spoke.

'He was so handsome. I remember thinking about how perfect his biceps were. They were big but they weren't so big that they looked... *cartoony*. Does that make any sense?'

'Sure,' replied Dave as he wrote the words *biceps not cartoony* on his notepad.

'I liked her straight away too,' said Hunter. 'She stood out.'

'So who made the first move?'

'I don't really remember. It was so long ago wasn't it? I know we swapped phone numbers but we didn't kiss that night at the club,' said Ella wistfully. 'I was so shy back then. I wouldn't have made the first move.'

Hunter nodded in agreement.

'I took her to an Italian place. Ella has always liked Italian food.'

'That's true! What was the name of that place in Bondi that we used to order from?'

'Da Orazio's pizza?' asked Hunter.

'Yes! Are they still around?'

Nobody in the room was sure and so they moved on with the interview. Ella retold all of the details that she could remember from their dinner together. She spoke very highly of a memorable chocolate brownie that she'd had for dessert. Ella informed Dave that it was during that dinner that Hunter revealed himself to be a professional wrestler.

'I didn't know what to say at first,' she added.

'It's a lot to take in I suppose. But I wanted to be honest with Ella straight away. If she wasn't going to be supportive of my passion then it wasn't going to work.'

'So Ella did you watch any professional wrestling before you met Hunter?' asked Dave.

'Goodness no. I'd never seen anything like it. It was all completely new to me.'

'Ella took a really long time to learn the rules of wrestling too,' added Hunter.

'Can either of you give me an example… for the book?'

'Well,' Ella began, 'I didn't know why the crowds would chant certain things when they did. There was this one occasion that springs to my mind. Once everyone was chanting *heel* at Hunter and I had no clue what that meant.'

'She thought I should heel like a dog,' said Hunter with a grin.

Ella let out a silent laugh that made her body bounce up and down joyfully.

'I was terrible with the lingo for a really long time!'

'But after you started wrestling with Hunter you picked things up?' asked Dave as he confirmed his recorder was still working properly.

'No…after I started wrestling as Obsession it became even more confusing to me. At one stage I thought Hunter and I could both simultaneously win a championship belt.'

'How would that have worked?' said Hunter shaking his head.

Ella shrugged. 'I wanted us both to have belts! I didn't really know what having a championship belt meant, let alone how you could win one.'

Hunter gave his wife a gentle pat on the thigh. His love for her was written all over his face.

'Would you please tell me about Obsession? Where did that character come from?' Dave had been unable to find the answer in any of Ella's previous interviews. Obsession had travelled around with The Hunter on the independent wrestling circuit and then vanished. The character had been a flash in the pan. Dave had already made a mental note to ask for copies of the photographs that hung around them. He suspected that most of them had never been published anywhere.

'Honestly the idea of her just came to me one day. I was getting into the world of wrestling and I was falling in love with Hunter. It was all manifesting itself into a kind of obsession anyway so I guess I thought… why not?'

'How about you?' asked Dave looking over at Hunter, 'We're you becoming *obsessed* with Ella too?'

'In the beginning, when the relationship was still new, there was a lot about Ella I didn't know.' Hunter looked at his wife and gave a loaded smile as he continued. 'I wouldn't say I was obsessed with her then. In a lot of ways I barely knew her. Ella was a nurse… I didn't realise that for a long time… I was so preoccupied with myself and my wrestling that I didn't even know.'

'Were you working as a nurse before you started wrestling?' asked Dave.

'I had taken some time off and I had always intended to go back to my job but then I started wrestling with Hunter…and that was exciting. We went on the road together and it seemed like such an adventure,' replied Ella with a smile. 'I put nursing off for a while longer.'

'So…you were a qualified nurse but you loved wrestling?'

'Yes. It was thrilling once I started accompanying Hunter to the ring. And there was a time when I didn't think I'd go back to nursing. But after almost a year together Hunter and I…well… we broke up.'

The energy in the room shifted and they all fell silent. Ella gave a half smile and knew that she had caused the awkwardness. Hunter wasn't sure what to say. Dave paused the recorder when he saw how upset they both looked.

'Are you alright? If you don't want to talk about this we can jump ahead…'

Dave trailed off as his subject composed herself. Ella indicated that she was okay and the recorder was turned back on.

'It…it still upsets me because when we broke up…that's when…Hunter started to use drugs. *Abuse* drugs really. It makes me sad to think about those days.'

'Hunter? Would you tell me what you remember about that time?'
He was uncomfortable for the first time since the interview had begun. Ella's words had not been harsh or accusatory but they had certainly been effective in changing the tone of things for Hunter. Dave waited patiently for him to speak.
'The problem with that time in my life…the reason I was taking so many drugs was because of my back and my kidney. I'd sustained an injury and I didn't know how to manage it properly.'
'He should have taken a break from wrestling,' chimed in Ella.
Ella was speaking not only as a medical professional but also as a concerned paramour.
'I should have. But the crowds were wild and the feeling of winning was addictive,' added Hunter as a means of explanation.
'Would you say that you have an addictive personality Hunter?' asked Dave as he jotted down a note.
'Yes. I wouldn't have been able to admit that back then but I know it now.'
Hunter was quick to reply. He was being brutally honest. Hunter had evolved. He was in a better place now and could reflect on everything with fresh eyes.
Ella put her hand over Hunters and took over for him.
'I was working as a nurse again…after the break up… and Hunter would come by and see me. He was hanging out with a bad crowd at the time. There were so many random guys that I couldn't keep track. They all had forgettable names like Oliver and John. I couldn't tell that Hunter was taking drugs at first but his behavior had changed.'
'What was different?' prodded Dave. They were opening up now and all of this could be invaluable material for the book that he was being paid to write about them. There was so much to cover.
'Hunter was very aggressive…he wanted to have sex with me all the time.'

'Still do,' said Hunter with a smile.

'You weirdo,' she said playfully before continuing. 'It was flattering… and I liked being pursued by him again. It felt like we were starting again in a way. Like it was all new. But Hunter was putting my job in jeopardy. People at work were starting to talk. They could tell he was using. The other nurses thought he might be trying to steal from the hospital, or that I was stealing things for him.'

'What were you using Hunter? If you don't mind my asking.'

'You name it, I tried it. As a wrestler you could get your hands on anything at the gym,' said Hunter matter-of-factly.

Ella continued.

'I was worried about you though. There was a day when you introduced yourself to me as if you'd never met me before. I thought you were mucking around. You said your name was *Hunter Hunter*.'

'I don't remember that. But there is quite a bit that I don't remember from that period of my life.'

'He was telling people to call him Thunder instead of The Hunter in the ring too.'

'Why?' asked Dave.

'I don't know. I have no idea actually,' Hunter replied. 'Maybe I was trying out a new persona. Honestly…I couldn't tell you what I was thinking.'

'That was a hard time in our relationship,' said Ella as her lips tightened into a frown. 'And it got worse when Caleb came back into the picture.'

'Who was Caleb?' asked Dave.

'He was a man that I'd dated briefly. It was before Hunter and I were ever together. Caleb…and I didn't know this at the time…was stalking me after we broke up. He had been following Hunter and I from place to place when we wrestled. He was in the crowd watching us. It's so strange to think about now.'

'So what happened?'

'Well…Hunter and I had broken up. He was becoming a distraction at work and we weren't really in a healthy place. I took a break from working and moved back in with my family.'

Hunter didn't speak. It was clear that he wasn't going to be able to contribute much as his memory of that time seemed lost. After a contemplative pause Dave continued his interview.

'And Caleb left you alone after that?'

'No. He found me at my parents' place…' Ella took a deep breath. Even after all these years the tale of her stalker ex-boyfriend was still difficult to tell.

'He broke into the house and stole my handbag. Then he set fire to it and left it burning in the driveway.'

'That must have been scary,' said Dave.

'It was. To know he had been *inside* the house made me crazy. A short time after that Caleb was arrested. He confessed to everything. He said insane things like how he wanted to *be* me. Caleb was committed to a mental institution years ago. It took me a while but eventually I started feeling comfortable again. I took a self-defense class. I started working out. I walked *everywhere*. I was in amazing shape,' said Ella proudly.

'And is that when you got back into wrestling?'

'I was in and out of it casually. It wasn't anything serious. It just… wasn't really the same as it had felt before. It wasn't as fun.'

'And Hunter? What were you up to during this time?'

Hunter was uncomfortable. He scratched his chin and sighed before he spoke.

'I became…quite famous I suppose.'

'Overseas?' asked Dave.

'Yeah…'

'Tell me more about how that happened.'

'Well, I guess it started when I became the Australian Heavyweight Champion. I know it was fake but I felt proud of that achievement. The federation made me 'the man' basically. I was on T-shirts, I was an action figure and everyone wanted a piece of me. My gimmick changed. I became a good guy again and preached the importance of being drug free. It was a good fit for me because I was clean and sober. I knew what I was talking about. Everyone in the locker room respected that and nobody tried to give me anything.'

'And you were the champion for almost a year right?'

Hunter nodded.

'That's right. I was one of the most well known professional wrestlers in the world for about ten months,' he mused.

'But then you and the federation management had a falling out?'

'Yes we did. I had built up this kind of cult following. I had lots of kids and youths looking up to me. I was showing people that they could achieve their dreams at the highest level and that they could do it without using drugs. Then management thought it would be a good idea to change my character again. They wanted me to pretend to have a drug relapse and become a heel. I wouldn't do it and so they didn't renew my contract. I thought it was a bluff at the time but they were serious.'

'It's crazy isn't it? I can't believe they dropped you when you had helped them grow their brand so much,' said Ella.

'I got depressed about it for a time. Then I met a man named Greg Peters. He offered to sponsor me if I would compete in cage fighting overseas.'

'And did you think that the skills you had acquired in the ring were comparable to cage fighting?' asked Dave. 'How did you know it was something you'd be good at?'

'I don't know what I thought. I guess I figured I was invincible back then. I won my first few cage fights and I assumed that I'd keep winning,' said Hunter with a shrug. 'I was immature and I didn't really plan things out.'

'Where did you fight?'

'Singapore, Hong Kong, Russia…the fights were scheduled really close together. Sometimes only weeks apart. It was grueling. I loved travelling but I missed Ella all the time.'

'And Ella, were you in touch with Hunter during that time?'

'It was long distance,' said Ella with a secret smile. 'I knew that he was reinventing himself and I didn't want to interfere. Hunter had to prove to the world that he was more than just a professional wrestler.'

Behind Hunter there was a poster that was covered in Chinese symbols. It was an international advertisement for one of Hunter's cage fights. The man on the poster looked intense and unbeatable.

'Your cage fights were legendary Hunter. They had some of the biggest internationally televised audiences of the nineties,' stated Dave. 'Did you prefer it to professional wrestling?'

'I didn't *prefer* it… so to speak…it was just a different world. I was taking a beating and being paid handsomely for it. They loved me. It was a different kind of love though. It was more real because I think everyone knew I could get hurt. There were stakes. The audience was more invested, you know?'

'Sure.'

'It couldn't last forever though. The schedule was taking its toll. I had started taking pain medication in order to deal with it… and the jet lag… and the fact that I was training non-stop. Sometimes I felt like I lived at the gym.'

'Hunter always trained too much. I've told him that for years,' said Ella.

Hunter casually flexed his bicep in front of his wife's face. Here was a man that valued his body more than anything. It was his livelihood. He was in great shape for a sixty-year old man. His wife felt his bicep with both hands and swooned.

'That's what I thought,' said Hunter with a cheeky grin.

Dave smiled at the exchange.

'But you sustained an injury? Was that during one of these cage fights?'

'Yeah…I was cage fighting in Hong Kong and I was against this absolute beast. He and I had been pretty evenly matched for five rounds. In the sixth round I took a knee to the ribs that smashed three of them beyond repair. Mr. Alfred…do you know Mr. Alfred?'

'Yes,' replied Dave. 'People tell me he was the best wrestling coach in the world during the nineties. I've spoken to him already.'

'Well Mr. Alfred told me I was done. I wasn't going to be able to continue fighting.'

'How did that make you feel?'

'I was devastated really. Crushed. I'd lost my professional wrestling dream and then my international cage fighting career was over.'

'And did your ribs heal?'

'Not as well as I'd hoped. I had to spend some time in physical therapy and that meant I couldn't travel back to Australia right away.'

'You wanted to come back? Why? Was that to see Ella?' he asked, pen poised for a response.

'Do you remember when the Minister for Sport set up that wrestling tournament a few years ago?' asked Ella.

'I read about this,' replied Dave. 'It was widely criticised. I think the Minister had to stand down for wasting tax payer money.'

'Well…this will be a scoop for your book. I was competing in that tournament. I used my real name but nobody realised it was me. They all knew me best as Obsession and she hadn't appeared for a few years.'

'I had no idea…' said Dave.

'Nobody knew except for Hunter. I told him about it over the phone. He was so supportive that he hired me a female wrestling coach. He wanted to be there himself but he couldn't travel right away…as he said.'

'How did you do in the competition?'

'I won the first round and then…I don't know what happened. They say I was beaten like a baby but I can't remember the details. I had a concussion.'

Hunter held his wife's hand, interlocking their fingers once more.

'I flew back to surprise her but because of the concussion she couldn't even remember that I was there.'

'That's awful.'

'It's alright,' said Ella. 'It was such a long time ago now. That was when I took a step back and started to see what was important to me. I missed Hunter. It was time to stop fighting and settle down.'

'Speaking of settling down,' Dave said, 'I couldn't find any record of your wedding in my research. When did you two get married?'

'We tied the knot in secret. It was after I had been clean and sober for a year. Ella had been supporting me and on the anniversary of my sobriety I proposed to her.'

'It was so sweet.' When Ella smiled small wrinkles formed at the edges of her eyes. 'He told me he'd been with hundreds of girls but that none of them could hold a candle to me. Hunter told me he loved me and that he always would. I said yes, and we went to the courthouse together the next day.'

'Did you have a honeymoon?'

Ella looked at Hunter, prompting him to speak next.

'Not really. I was contacted by my sponsor Greg and I flew out to commence training about a week later. Ella was really good about it. She knew that the cage fighting opportunity was something I had to try.'

'And Hunter and I kept the wedding a secret from my family and from all of our friends. I have a big family and it was tough not to tell them. I'm really close with my sisters Jasmine and Sarah. We eventually had a proper wedding in front of everyone but that was years later.'

Ella caressed a golden necklace that had been resting around her neck.

'Okay so…let's jump ahead. What changed? Hunter - you were injured. Ella - you'd just lost that tournament. What brought you back into the limelight?'

'It was my old roommate Whiz. You might know him by his wrestling name Whiz Bang?'

'Yes I know him,' said Dave.

'Well Wizzy and I used to live together when we were coming up through the ranks. When he finally made his big television debut he wore a T-shirt that said *Hunter's Rush* during one of his first fights.'

'That was one of your old shirts?' enquired Dave.

'Yeah…it was a plain black promotional shirt that I used to wear sometimes.'

'And 'Hunter's Rush' referred to?'

'My finishing move. So Whiz wore this shirt and for some reason people wanted to know the significance. He did a promo about me and then someone from the company got in touch. Before I knew it I was accompanying him to the ring.'

'Fantastic,' said Dave with a smile. 'Lucky he wore that shirt.'

'Well back when I lived with him it was a good day if he wore anything at all!'

'Whiz was something of an exhibitionist,' said Ella.

'It was as if he was allergic to cotton,' added Hunter.

Dave grinned and wrote a note for himself. He'd have to interview the man that inadvertently relaunched Hunter's career in the near future.

'So people were talking about you again?'

'Yes. It was a snowball effect. Some of my old fights went viral. People seemed to love them. Suddenly my old manager Ian got in touch. Everyone wanted to interview me again.' Hunter's face lit up as he spoke. 'It was as if it was all meant to happen that way. I took so many detours but I still wound up in the world of wrestling in the end.'

'And you became a fan favourite right away. I've been watching back some of the footage of your return. How did that feel?' asked Dave with a grin.

'I was crying…you know? I couldn't hold it in. I had to wait a lifetime but when eighty thousand plus are cheering for you? Forget it. It was one of the greatest moments of my life.'

'You deserved it honey. You've always been a wrestling legend. It just took that night to make you see it for yourself,' Ella announced proudly.

'Thank you. You're being too sweet though. You're going to make me cry again.' Ella chuckled to herself.

'After Hunter started appearing as Whiz Bang's manager for a while the company set him up as a kind of wrestling trainer character. He started to 'hunt out' fresh talent in the wrestling roster and then they'd film him training them…'

'I'd accompany them to the ring and cheer them on. That sort of thing.'

'Then after a couple of years the writers came up with a storyline for me. This punk kid called Mikey Cross came out and challenged my credentials. He said I was a phony and then he introduced his trainer, who he claimed was the real thing.'

'And that's when Buster came out?'

'That's right. I hadn't seen him in years. He looked good. Buster had stayed in shape and he'd been working on and off in the independent circuits.'

'And they had signed Buster to work with you?'

'Yeah… they had this whole storyline planned out. Buster and Cross were going to challenge me and Wizzy. I didn't really have to wrestle but I took a few good bumps to sell the storyline.'

'And that wasn't too much for you? Were your ribs alright?'

'Oh yeah. By that time my ribs were really manageable. I didn't have to exert myself too much. They all made me look good. The crowd liked it too.'

'And how did the feud end?'

'We had a match…a cage match ironically… between Whiz and Cross. The winning trainer would get to stay and the losing trainer had to resign. Whiz won for me and I got to stick around for a while.'

Dave took a picture out of his folder of notes. In it Ella was standing next to Hunter. He'd found the image in a recently published wrestling magazine.

'Tell me about this picture Ella.'

'That's from the night Hunter was inducted into the Hall of Fame.'

'I had no idea they were going to do that by the way,' said Hunter. 'After the feud, in order to make sure nobody could challenge my credentials again, they inducted me into the Hall of Fame. I couldn't believe it when they told me. They brought Buster back for the night and he gave me the award.'

'It was the most amazing experience,' said Ella.

Hunter composed himself. Dave could tell he was trying not to cry.

'I was a poor kid. My father died when I was younger because we couldn't afford medicine for him. I fell in with a bad crowd. I used to get in street fights when I was a kid. If you'd told me back then that I would be known worldwide for fighting I would never have believed you.'

'If you weren't a fighter what would you be doing?'

'He made a lousy waiter, I'll tell you that much,' said Ella with a laugh.

'I was just trying to get the girls as drunk as possible.'

'Well you were good at *that*,' she retorted.

'If I wasn't wrestling? Who knows! I could have been in jail...or worse. I didn't really have a plan. I was living from one day to the next.'

'And now you two are enjoying your retirement. So are you both done with wrestling now?'

'You're never really *done* with professional wrestling. Even when you're old and grey they still bring you out for nostalgia. They give you something easy to do backstage or they make you general manager for the night or they have you accompany some young buck that needs a push to the ring. Wrestling is for life. I'll be done with wrestling when I'm dead,' said Hunter.

Dave found their banter fascinating. They talked about their favourite rivalries and moments they'd shared on the road. Hunter brought out newspaper clippings and old interviews from the beginning of his career. The couple seemed completely at ease with eachother. It was as if they had fought a lifetime's worth of arguments already and now at last they were free to enjoy one another's company.

'Before you go I was wondering if you had given any thought to a title for our book?' asked Ella.

'I feel like the title of this book might be *Fighting for Love* or *Ecstasy of the Heart*... or something like that. The publishers want a title that captures both the relationship as well as the wrestling aspect.'

'That sounds kind of sappy to me,' replied Hunter. 'That's just a *working* title right? You're going to come up with something better?'

'With your help I will. We're going to get together alot more. I want this book to reflect everything that happened accurately.'

'Not *too* accurately I hope,' said Ella and her eyes lit up. 'Do you remember that fight we had about the sandwich honey?'

The couple shared another knowing smile.

'The sandwich? Is that something that's worth including in the book?' asked Dave.

'Oh goodness no,' replied Ella. 'It was one of the silliest fights we've ever had. I can't imagine anyone wanting to read about something like that.'

Dave furrowed his brow and adjusted his glasses again.

'Well, tell me something that the readers *would* want to know about? Before I go.'

Ella thought for a moment.

'Hunter likes Ed Sheeran. And he knew about his music before anyone.'

'Okay… that's… *something*. How about a fact that nobody knows. Something personal?' he asked.

'I always steal Hunter's shirts,' she said proudly.

'That's true actually,' said Hunter with a chuckle.

'Why is that?' the ghostwriter asked.

'It's the smell. It's the feeling of being close to him. I can't explain it but it's something I've always done with him. I think he likes it when I wear his clothes too.'

Hunter nodded in agreement.

'You two haven't been very public together. This book is going to shine a light on your personal lives in a way you might not be ready for. I hope that's okay?'

'Oh of course. Hunter and I expected that. What's the point of living such a big life if you can't share the journey with the people that helped you along the way? We wanted to tell our story now while we're still here to tell it. And it was such an adventure! Adventures are made to be shared.'

'How did you deal with the time apart when Hunter was travelling and fighting? Didn't you worry about him?'

'It was impossible not to. He was my husband. We wrote to eachother while we were apart. I have hundreds of letters and postcards from Hunter.'

'Could I take a look at those?' asked Dave raising his eyebrow. This was another priceless resource.

'Sure,' said Ella as she left the room. She returned carrying a metal tin that was full of old correspondence. Preserved inside were postcards from all over the world. There were candid photographs and notes scribbled on hotel stationary.

'This is amazing. Please…please tell me I can include some of these in the book,' said Dave with wide pleading eyes.

'Of course you can!' said Hunter. 'Just tell me which ones you want to use. I'd like to make sure I sound as good as I look.'

As the sun was setting the interview concluded and Dave packed up his recorder and notepads that were now filled with details, leads and ideas.

'So what happens now?' asked Ella as they walked him to the front door of their Australian home.

'Well I'll head back to my hotel room and write an outline of your story. Then we'll flesh it out over the next few months together.'

'And we're just meant to trust you? How do we know *what* you're going to write?' mused Hunter as he folded his muscular arms.

'Well I suppose you could write it yourself if you want,' said Dave with a smile. The couple chuckled at the notion.

'I think we'll leave this one to you,' said Ella with a smile. 'Try not to make us sound stupid.'

'I'll do my best. Thanks Hunter…Ella. It was so nice to spend this time with you.'

'You too Dave. All the best,' nodded Hunter and they shook hands.

Ella hugged the writer goodbye.

'I've got a good feeling about this,' she said with a smile.

Dave walked down the driveway towards the mailbox. It was so nice and tranquil here, an hour outside of Sydney, that he couldn't help feeling at ease. He placed the recorder inside his jacket pocket and unlocked his car. In his mind he tried to imagine the best way to tell the story of Hunter and Ella. He'd been charmed by how happy they seemed together. Both had been wrestling royalty in their heyday. Hunter and Ella were known worldwide. Between them they had helped to inspire a generation of youths. Dave wanted to do their amazing story justice. This book was going to be a big deal for them all.

As he started the engine of his car he spotted Hunter at the window and gave him a wave. Hunter nodded and closed the blinds. This felt like a story that had to be shared and the writer would do his best to give them the ending they deserved.

## A WORD FROM THE AUTHOR

This wasn't a book I had ever *really* intended on writing. I mean… yes – I had an idea and it has made its way into a novel – but it wasn't meant to be *this* idea exactly. I sort of feel like I've made lemonade out of lemons!

I liked the idea of fictionalising a romantic comedy about professional wrestling and thought about turning that into a screenplay more than anything. It just happened to be the idea on the tip of my brain when I booked that first ghostwriter to do the initial work. Strangely, I now feel the story of Hunter and Ella is complete. I have no desire to write it as a screenplay at all! Although imagining it as a film based on *this* book makes me laugh. Imagine actors delivering the words *exactly* as written! This was basically a personal joke that got out of hand. And in a lot of ways this might be the worst novel ever written. But I'm glad I saw this writing experiment through to the end.

I think the lesson of *Dropping the Belt* is obvious. Don't cut creative corners! Don't pay someone to do something that you can do yourself. You'll find the journey of writing a novel far more satisfying if you do it one page at a time. That was my experience with *The Glove* anyway.

The Internet is an odd place. People can claim to be anything out there. If you hand over your money all you can do is hope for the best. You'll probably never see it again. I guess I was lucky to get something that made me laugh and brought me some joy.

I suppose I'm also publishing this as a cautionary tale. If you're reading a story one day and it's called 'Ecstasy of the Heart' or it bears a striking resemblance to the work featured in this book – you'll know.

You will know that there are a limited number of story templates that these online 'writers' use. And you'll realise that they are still recycling them. It's not something that I have the time or resources to prove but I suspect that ghostwriting doesn't always produce original work.

I'm glad something tangible could come from this experience. It would have been depressing to hand over a sum of money without having anything to show for it. Hopefully dear reader you found the journey more enjoyable than frustrating!

And now some praise for the people that were instrumental in the making of this book. A big thank you to my wonderful wife Tess, who endured my dealings with these ghostwriters in real time. You were patient and supportive as always while I went crazy and let this project consume me. I love you. It was a funny and sometimes frustrating learning experience that has highlighted the dangers of asking others to write for you.

My thanks to my friends who read the work of the first ghostwriter and couldn't get through it all! Thanks for letting me know I had something really special. Your laughter helped me realise the potential of this comedic endeavour. And a big thank you to all of the PWA professional wrestlers from my 2008 documentary *The Young and The Wrestlers* who planted the seeds of this project in my mind.

Special thanks should be reserved for Kane 'Mikey' Broadrick – who inspired the idea when he worked as a topless waiter. Sometimes a throw away comment has a ripple effect even a decade later.

And finally a huge thank you to my younger brother William who stayed up watching wrestling with me and fanned the flame of my interest for years to come. He wasn't the only brother who sat and watching wrestling over the years – there was Tom, Adam, Edward, Nick and Robert – but he was there through the majority of it. And Will was happy to dedicate hours of his time storytelling with me. I'll always remember it fondly.

Thanks for reading along on this rollercoaster with me. I've read over *Dropping the Belt* so many times now that it's hard to know whether it's actually funny anymore. As I said I hope you found some amusement along the way.

If you liked the book (or even if you didn't!) I hope you'll take a moment to rate it on Amazon or share it with a friend so that others might find it too. You can source my other books there as well if you're interested. They are nothing like this.

Cheers.<br>David Farrell

About the Author.

David Farrell lives in Melbourne with his wife and children.

He has Directed two independent feature films and has a film Podcast called *Pod Me If You Can*.

His stories *The Last Resort*, *Twelve* and *The Glove* are available now on Amazon. His children's story *You Can't Get Rid of Me That Easily* is also available now.

You can contact him @DaveFarrell1 on Twitter.

www.ingramcontent.com/pod-product-compliance
Lightning Source LLC
Chambersburg PA
CBHW052028070526
44584CB00016B/1949